Julia Bird's Soft Furnishings

For Arthur Slack, who endured it all

First published in 1996
Conran Octopus Limited
37 Shelton Street
London WC2H 9HN

British Library Cataloguing-in-Publication Data.
A catalogue record for this book is available from the British Library.

ISBN 1 85029 840 8

Editorial Director: Suzannah Gough
Project Editor: Alison Bolus
In-house Editor: Jenna Jarman
Art Editor: Georgina Rhodes
Photographer: Pia Tryde
Illustrator: Carolyn Jenkins
Production Controller: Jill Beed
Typeset by Richard Proctor
Printed in Hong Kong

CREATIVE PROJECTS for the HOME

Julia Bird's Soft Furnishings

PHOTOGRAPHY by PIA TRYDE

CONRAN OCTOPUS

CONTENTS

INTRODUCTION

Ever since I was a little girl I have had a passion for fabric. My mother was a keen seamstress and would always donate the remnants from her most recent sewing project to my collection. Pretty cotton prints, sturdy woven tweeds, shiny modern nylons and scraps of lace – I coveted them all. Each piece would be cherished, awaiting transformation into new furnishings for my dolls' house. The results of those formative years have led to this book, which reflects my enthusiasm for the dynamics of colour, pattern, fabric and for experimenting with ideas.

The basic concept was to create a wide selection of simple, practical soft furnishing ideas that were inspirational, essentially achievable and well suited to today's contemporary lifestyle. With the combination of clear step-by-step instructions and illustrations my intention was to encourage the reader to feel confident enough to attempt projects that might initially seem daunting, but that are in fact relatively easy to tackle. Some designs are so basic that even the most reticent needleworker will feel motivated; others will provide a challenge for those more accomplished on the sewing front.

I have included a wide range of furnishing items made up in a diverse selection of fabrics, chosen to illustrate the effectiveness of combining various colours, patterns and textures. Despite the extensive choice of beautiful fabrics available today, I still find myself returning to those familiar basics that are generally inexpensive and easily available: calico, muslin, denim, cotton canvas, gingham and natural linen. All look great on their own, and all can be worked into something dynamically original by the application of traditional sewing techniques such as embroidery, appliqué, pleating, patchwork and quilting.

Each of the main projects in this book includes a 'Do it Differently' section in which I provide suggestions for developing the idea further. There is a limit to what can be shown in this book, of course, but with a little imagination one can easily adapt a design to suit a different look or lifestyle. There are no hard and fast rules, and what appeals to one person will not necessarily suit another. What is important, though, is a willingness to experiment. Part of the process of creating something new and original involves a willingness to experiment and, inevitably, make the occasional mistake. Expensive mistakes – particularly those involving curtains, with large amounts of material required – can be minimized by the use of old sheets or lengths of calico to try out new designs. Another useful practice is to work small samplers to test appliqué or embroidery stitches so that the choice of colour, texture and weights of varying threads can be perfected.

A combination of imagination and experimentation, together with the basic sewing skills, is all that is required; then there are surely no limits to the original and exciting results possible.

FELT *flower* CUSHION

Hard-wearing wool baize is perfectly suitable for these large, comfy cushions, while felt is the ideal choice to provide the scalloped trim and the decorative appliqué. It is easy to be inspired by the glorious range of colours in which you can buy felt. Brilliant orange, mauve and chestnut brown were chosen to decorate the smaller cushion, with some flowers and leaves enlivened with simple stitching in contrasting embroidery threads.

❧

MATERIALS

Wool fabric for cushion cover (wool baize is strong and inexpensive) • Coloured felts • Basting thread • Matching sewing thread • Iron-on interfacing (two strips measuring 5cm/2in x width of cushion) • Matching stranded cotton embroidery threads

EQUIPMENT

In addition to the basic kit (see page 138), you will need: Button approx. 2cm/¾in in diameter for template • Small sharp scissors • Paper • Embroidery needle

1 Measure the length and width of the cushion to be covered, adding an extra 1.5cm (⅝in) for seam allowances all around, and use these measurements to cut out the front section of the cover. Cut two sections for the back, each measuring the width of the cushion but only half its length; add an extra 10cm (4in) to the length (1.5cm/⅝in seam allowance, 6cm/2⅜in hem and 2.5cm/1in overlap) and an extra 3cm (1¼in) to the width.

2 To make the scalloped edge trimming, cut some strips of felt, about 4cm (1½in) wide, and use a tailor's pencil and the half-circumference of the button to draw a row of half circles (fig. 1). (Choose the size of the button in accordance with the size of the scallop wanted.) Then cut carefully along the pencil lines and also trim along the top edge of the strip to leave a 2cm (¾in) margin above the scallops.

3 Pin and baste the scalloped felt around all four edges of the right side of the front section (see Notes), raw edges together. Ease the felt gently around the corners. Because of felt's flexibility, the scalloped strips will probably not need to be clipped at the corners in the way that piping would. Machine stitch in place, taking care to stitch close to the top of the scallops. Trim the corners and seams (fig. 2).

4 Fold 1cm (3/8in) and then 5cm (2in) to the wrong side on one width edge of both back sections, and press. Unfold the hems and insert a strip of iron-on interfacing into each to lie between the fold lines. Fold the hems back in position, so that the interfacing is sandwiched inside, and press them in place, following the iron-on interfacing manufacturer's instructions. Machine stitch the hems close to the folded edge. Mark two or three buttonholes in the middle of one section, and machine or hand stitch them.

5 Now cut out paper templates of a flower, a stem and a leaf motif (using either the designs provided here or some of your own). Lay them on the coloured felt and cut out a series of each. Arrange the felt flowers, stems and leaves on the front section, using the scalloped border as a frame, and then pin them in place. Now stitch them using the embroidery thread and stem stitch (see Stitch Directory) (fig. 3).

6 When the design is complete, pin the back sections to the front, right sides together. Make sure that the buttonholed back section lies beneath the other one; they should overlap by 5cm (2in) (fig. 4). Pin, baste and machine stitch in place, following the stitching line. Turn right side out and press. Finally, sew on the required number of buttons in the centre of the section underneath the buttonholes.

NOTES

❧ The scalloped edge does not need to be made in a single long piece. Smaller sections can be pieced together when you pin them in place, as the final stitching line will reveal only the actual scallop and not the joins.

❧ When stitching your flower, stem and leaf motifs in place, it is more effective to use a contrasting coloured thread to that of the felt being stitched. You can split the thread into three strands for more delicate work.

❧ If the wool fabric is thick, you might find that the seam is too bulky and does not sit neatly when the cover is turned right side out. If this happens, trim the layers of wool and felt that form the seam allowance to slightly different widths for a flatter finish.

fig. 1

fig. 2

fig. 3

fig. 4

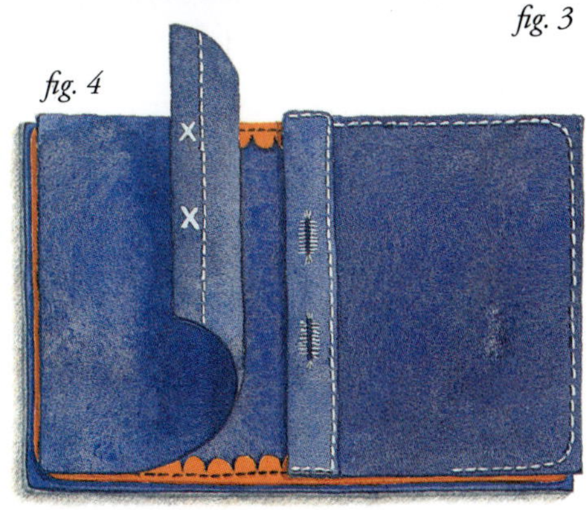

DO IT *differently*

Felt possesses certain qualities that make it the perfect craft fabric. It is easy to work with, does not fray and responds to dyes exceptionally well – as is evident in the wonderful range of richly saturated colours in which it can be bought.

FAR LEFT *An alternative to the hand-embroidered appliqué that features on the cushions is to machine stitch around the outer edge of the motif. This is a lot easier if the design is fairly simple and free flowing, as demonstrated in these swirly patterned book covers. It is best to glue your design lightly in place using fabric glue. Once the glue has dried, carefully machine stitch close to the edge. If your proposed design is more complicated, and you feel you are unlikely to be able to control the speed of the sewing machine, then it is possible simply to glue the design in place. This would not, however, be suitable if the item is likely to have plenty of use, because the edges will inevitably peel away; in such cases, stitch the design in place by hand, using blanket stitch or stem stitch (see Stitch Directory).*

LEFT *Here, the same scalloped edging that trimmed the cushions and throw has been used to enhance a pair of mauve ticking-stripe curtains. The scalloped edging, in a lively lizard green, was cut in exactly the same way and sewn in place along the curtain edge. The lining fabric was then stitched on to the reverse of the curtains, following the previous stitching line. In the same way, you could continue the theme by trimming the edge of a matching pelmet (valance) and tie-backs.*

CONTRAST *cushion* COVERS

It is the playful interchange of colour, checks and floral pattern that transforms these very basic tie-on cushion covers into something really special. Each cover boasts a series of ties that secure the closing end, while revealing a cushion lining cover made from a contrasting fabric. Cushions covered in this manner are effortless to make and are a useful way of linking up colour schemes with other furnishings in the room.

MATERIALS

Two contrasting fabrics (enough of each to cover both sides of the cushion, plus extra for ties [optional], see step 3) • Coloured or plain tape/ribbon • Basting thread • Matching sewing thread

EQUIPMENT

Basic kit (see page 138)

1 Measure the width and length of the cushion or pillow. Cut two pieces of one of the fabrics to these measurements, adding 2cm (¾in) to three of the sides for seam allowances and 6cm (2½in) to the fourth side for the opening. With wrong sides together, sew French seams (see Techniques) along the three sides, stitching 1cm (⅜in) in both times. Press.

2 Now, with the right sides still together, turn under double 3cm (1¼in) hems on both opening edges. Press. Sew along both edges to complete, then press again.

3 Now hand sew pairs of tape or ribbon ties at equal and opposite points along the opening. If you would prefer to make your own ties in matching or contrasting fabric, cut four strips measuring 20 x 4cm (8 x 1½in). Fold both long edges into the centre (wrong sides together) of each strip. Then fold each strip in half, turning in the ends as you do so, and machine stitch across the ends and along the side.

4 Finally, cut and stitch the contrasting cushion cover in exactly the same way, and slip it on top of the previous cover in the opposite direction. The cushion covers are, naturally, interchangeable.

NOTES

❧ It is usually best (although not essential) to use contrasting fabrics of roughly the same weight.

❧ If you don't want to see the base fabric through the top cover, use a denser or darker fabric on top. For an idea on letting the base colour show through the top cover, see page 21.

❧ Why not have openings and ties at both ends? Simply complete French seams along two sides of each cushion and adjust the length of the cut fabric to accommodate an extra hem (i.e. two sides will have 2cm/¾in seam allowances and two will have 6cm/2½in). Turn up double hems on two opposite sides, and make double the number of ties in matching or contrasting fabrics.

fig. 1

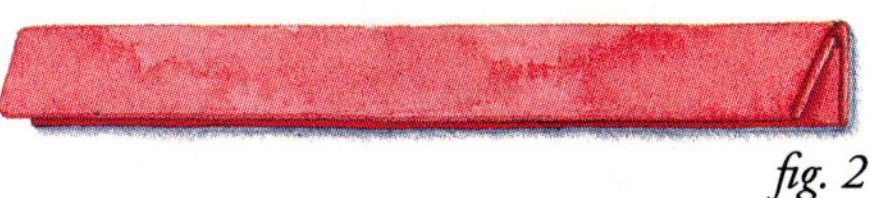

fig. 2

fig. 3

DO IT *differently*

As these cushion or pillow covers are so simple to make, you can have a wonderful time experimenting with different combinations of fabric and various styles of openings. If you want both fabrics to be seen, try an outer cover of organza, which will allow the base colour to show through.

FAR LEFT *Chinese-style fastenings are a more unusual way of securing a cushion, and are relatively simple to make. You will need two long, thin lengths of fabric, approximately 4 x 40cm (1½ x 16in), rolled to form a long tube, with the raw edge turned in and hand sewn in place. (The length will depend on how big you want the coils to be, so it is worth practising first.) For the 'button' side, tie a Turk's head knot in the middle of one length (see Stitch Directory). Now, starting from each end, coil the remaining fabric closely on either side of the knot. Check the size of the coils and, if you are happy with them, unravel them, then rewind them, stitching them in place as you go along. If they are too big, trim the ends before rewinding them.*
For the 'buttonhole' side, take the second length of rolled fabric, mark the middle, and from this point create a loop that will just fit over the Turk's head knot. Secure the loop with a few stitches. Then coil and stitch both ends, as before. Your Chinese-style fastening is now ready to sew in place on the opening of the cushion cover.

LEFT *Organza is always interesting to work with, and here its subtle gauzy translucence effectively subdues the brightly coloured fabric beneath, while providing a cool, smooth surface on top. Such a pillow would be the perfect foil to a hot summer's night. Covered buttons (finished with a layer of organza) and matching fabric loops create a neat, tailored finish.*

PATCHWORK *armchair* COVER

This pretty armchair has been loosely covered with pieces of old French mattress ticking, salvaged and patchworked together, resulting in a lovely, old-fashioned, country look. Ticking fabrics are designed to be hard-wearing, and by reworking the undamaged parts of these mattress covers we created a unique fabric that is strong and should last well.

MATERIALS

Enough material to make up panels of patchwork to cover the chair • Basting thread • Matching sewing thread • Touch-and-close tape

EQUIPMENT

In addition to the basic kit (see page 138), you will need: Upholstery pins (extra long with large head)

1 Measure your chair so that you have rough dimensions for all the sections of the cover: back, front, arms, sides, arm fronts, seat base and seat front. Allow for a 1.5cm (⅝in) seam around all the edges, except those that join the seat panel, where an extra 10cm (4in) will be needed along three sides of the seat so that the material can be tucked in neatly. Decide on your patchwork design, and make up panels of fabric pieces to fit each section generously, allowing an extra 5cm (2in) for the hem, where required. Press all the patchwork seams flat (fig. 1, below).

2 Now pin the panels to the chair – right sides showing – using upholstery pins placed along the outer edges of each panel, and ensuring that the fabric lies flat and that the pattern is neatly centred (fig. 2). Trim the edges, bearing in mind the extra 10cm (4in) seam allowance around the seat. Work around each panel of the chair until all the panels are pinned in place.

3 Pin the seam allowances together (see Notes). Open out each pinned seam allowance in turn and mark the proposed seamline with tailor's pencil on the wrong side of the fabric. Replace the pins. Where the seams are curved, snip regularly around the corners to ease the tension (fig. 3).

4 Now take out all the upholstery pins and remove the cover from the chair. Invert all the seams, pin by pin, using the tailor's markings as a guideline and matching any notches, so that the cover is turned inside out. The right sides of the fabric should now be together ready for sewing. Leave a gap along one seam where the back meets the side, up to about halfway. Test to see how big to make it by trying the cover on the chair. Sew strips of touch-and-close tape in place.
Baste and machine stitch the seams, then trim them neatly. Zigzag stitch the edges to prevent fraying. Press the seams, then turn the cover right side out. Place it over the chair and mark the required position for the hem. Remove the cover and turn under the hem. Pin, baste and machine stitch, then press.

NOTES

❧ Once the seam allowances are pinned, you can determine the tightness of the cover's fit. Ours was made up slightly loosely for a more contemporary, comfortable look; for a tighter fit, simply pin the seams accordingly.

❧ The design of some chairs is such that a loose cover can be pulled on and off without any opening being needed. Most, however, will require some form of opening. Follow the method outlined in step 4 – using both side seams if necessary. Alternatively, split the back panel in half (two extra seam allowances will have to be added), and finish with ties or covered buttons and loops to create an interesting design detail at the back (fig. 4).

❧ We have shown the simplest look, without any piping detail. If you would like to highlight certain outlines with piping, make up the required lengths of piping (see Techniques) and insert them when the seams are being re-pinned inside out. The piping will then be basted and stitched with the seams.

fig. 2

fig. 3

fig. 4

DO IT *differently*

Patchwork presents a good opportunity to recycle lovely old bits of fabric you cannot bear to throw away. Patchwork need not involve complicated designs and laborious work: simple strips of fabric can be just as effective. What is important is your choice of colours and their combined effect.

FAR LEFT *Covered buttons make an excellent decorative finish to patchwork cushions. When covering buttons, cut out the circle of fabric and embroider it first. It may be necessary to line the fabric with a fine iron-on interfacing to ensure that the metal button does not show through.*

LEFT *The cushions shown here are made of strips of richly iridescent velvet pieced together, with embroidered stitches in coloured threads decorating the seams. The central back opening was finished with covered buttons embroidered to match. A variety of embroidery stitches can be used to finish off the patchwork seams in a decorative manner. Here, herringbone stitch is demonstrated, with stars embellishing the buttons. Other options include feather, chain, cross or fly stitch (see Stitch Directory).*

TAILORED *chair* COVER

All styles of dining chair can benefit from a smartly tailored cover. Here a plain chair has been dramatically transformed into a stylish dining chair by the addition of a close-fitting cover. The strong design of the fabric is further enhanced by a contrasting gingham check panel and piping. Choose your cover style to suit your chair: close fitting and well piped for a shapely chair, looser and less formal for a plain one.

MATERIALS

Plain fabric (see step 1 to calculate quantity) • Contrasting fabric for trim and piping • Basting thread • Matching sewing thread • Piping cord to run around seat and chair back

EQUIPMENT

In addition to the basic kit (see page 138), you will need: Machine piping foot

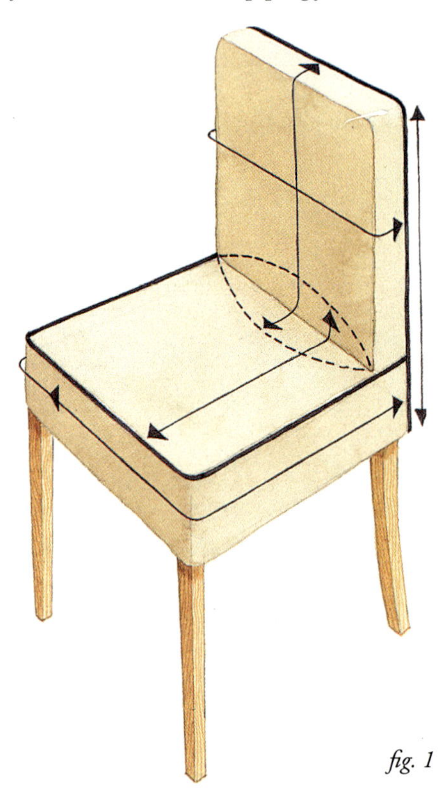

fig. 1

1 Measure each section – front, back and seat (fig. 1) – and add a 2.5cm (1in) seam allowance all around, plus an extra 5cm (2in) on the bottom edge of the back section. Curve out the back of the seat and the bottom of the front section by about 5cm (2in) to allow some 'give'. Cut out each piece.

Measure around the seat to the back for the skirt width. Allow double the length required if you are using lightweight fabric (as shown here), otherwise add a hem allowance of 5cm (2in). Cut it as one long piece (if you can).

2 Make enough piping (see Techniques), using the contrasting fabric cut on the cross, to edge around three sides of the seat and around the top and sides of the back, reaching down to the bottom of the skirt. Turn in and press a 2.5cm (1in) seam allowance on all the pieces, then unfold them. Now apply one length of the piping along the folded line of the back section (see Techniques), stopping at the hem allowance on each side.

3 Pin and baste the back and front sections, right sides together (making darts in the top corners of the front to accommodate the thickness of the chair back). Machine stitch all around the edge as closely as possible to the line of piping stitching. Turn right side out and press (fig. 2).

4 Pin and baste the curved edges of the seat and front sections, right sides together, and machine stitch up to the seam allowance. Now apply the remaining piping to the seat, up to the basted seam. Short lengths will be left on each side to extend to the back seam (fig. 3). Hand stitch these along the front section where it extends to the back.

5 Fold the skirt panel in half widthways and press. The folded edge will become the finished hem of the skirt. Cut (on the cross) a 7cm (2¾in) wide strip of contrasting fabric to the width of the skirt panel. Turn in 1cm (⅜in) along both sides and press, to leave a 5cm (2in) wide strip. Pin and baste in position, 2.5cm (1in) from the hem edge. Stitch in place and press.

6 Now pin and baste the seat and skirt sections, right sides together, along the piping. Ease a gentle curve around the front corners, and clip these. Now stitch as closely as possible to the line of the piping stitching. Trim, then zigzag all seam edges. Turn right sides out and press (fig. 4).
Finally, hand stitch both sides of the skirt to the back section along the line of piping. The hem of the skirt should be level with the bottom edge of the piping; hem the back section to align with the skirt hem.

NOTES

❧ Fit the cover over the chair at every single stage for a perfect fit. Upholstery is often uneven in places; a generous seam allowance permits adjustments.

❧ If your cover needs an opening to slip it on and off the chair, see page 25 for some ideas on fastening.

❧ A cover in a lightweight fabric will need to be fully lined. Cut out all the pieces from the lining then treat main and lining fabrics as one single layer.

fig. 2

fig. 3

fig. 4

DO IT *differently*

Without altering the basic technique of making a chair cover, you can engineer different effects by changing certain elements. The skirt can have ruffles or pleats, or be made longer or shorter; the hem can be finished with a scalloped or zigzagged edge (for which the skirt will need to lined), and piping can be matching or contrasting.

FAR LEFT *Effective and decorative means of closure – including ties fashioned into bows or knots, and buttons fastened into button holes or loops – can become prominent features of the cover.*

LEFT *The generous, flirty ruffle shown here was achieved by doubling the width of the skirt, and then gathering it to fit. If you prefer a pleated skirt, it is best to pleat one section of the fabric and from this calculate how much extra fabric is being used; you can then extend the skirt as necessary. The gathering, pleating or any fancy hem should all be completed before the skirt is attached to the seat section. A scalloped or zigzag finish along the hem are other decorative options (for which the skirt will need to be lined).*

EXOTIC *tasselled* BOLSTER

A pair of bolster cushions make perfect rests on a day bed and are a stylish alternative to the more usual pile of squashy cushions. Indian silks woven with threads of gold and iridescent colours inspired the making of these very simple covers. A contrasting fabric is used to add definition to the bolster ends, and the drawstrings of thin gold cord are finished with a matching gold tassel.

❧

MATERIALS

Main fabric and contrasting fabric (see step 1 to calculate quantities) • Approx. 2m (2¼yd) gold cord • 2 gold tassels • Basting thread • Matching sewing thread

EQUIPMENT

In addition to the basic kit (see page 138), you will need: Safety pin

1 Measure around the bolster cushion for the width, and from end to end of the bolster for the length; add 5cm (2in) to both measurements for seam allowances. Use these measurements to mark and cut a length of material from the main fabric.

Cut two sections from the contrasting fabric. The width of each will be the same as for the main fabric; the length of each (which will be shorter than the width) will be equal to the radius of the bolster, plus 5cm (2in) for seam allowances (fig. 1).

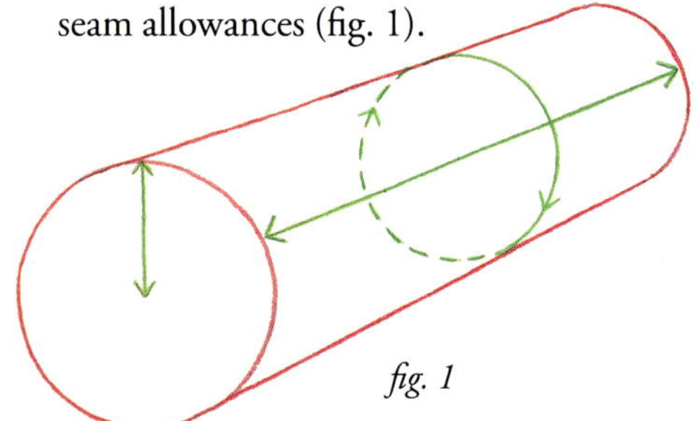

fig. 1

2 Pin, baste and machine stitch one contrasting section to each end of the main section, right sides together, using 2.5cm (1in) seams. Then pin, baste and machine stitch along the full length of all three fabric sections, right sides together, to make a long tube,

again using a 2.5cm (1in) seam. Leave a 1cm (⅜in) gap at each end of the long seam, set 2.5cm (1in) in from the edge (fig. 2). These gaps will become the eyelets through which to thread the gold cord.

3 Turn in a 2.5cm (1in) hem at each end of the tube, and pin, baste and machine stitch the hem in place. The eyelet hole at each end should sit on the outside of the cover, in between the fold and the stitching line. Press and turn right side out (fig. 3). Thread half your selected length of cord through each eyelet (1m/39in provides a more than generous bow). The easiest way to do this is to attach one end of the cord to a safety pin, close the pin, then thread it through the channel.
Push the bolster cushion into the cover from one end, and, when it is in place, pull the cords to gather in each end. Attach the tassels as you secure the cords with knots.

NOTES

❧ Experiment with different kinds of fabric. Try using a single striped fabric, but with the stripes running in the opposite direction for the contrasting fabric ends.

❧ For a more structured effect, try incorporating piping or a fancy trim within the seams that join the main and contrasting fabric pieces.

❧ Remember that bulky fabrics will not gather up as efficiently as finer ones, leaving a gaping hole at each end. This could be used as a feature, if the bolster is covered with a suitably matching or contrasting lining.

fig. 2 *fig. 3*

DO IT *differently*

There are various other ways of making bolster covers, and your choice will depend on how decorative you want them to look. A plainer effect than the drawstring can be achieved by leaving the ends ungathered and finishing them with a circular piece of fabric. Contrasting piping around the edge adds interesting detail.

LEFT *Should you choose to gather the ends, there are various options for the closing. One is to make a long tie – one half in one colour, the other half in another colour, or using two colours of ribbon sewn together – and to thread it through the channel and tie it off in a series of bows on top of one another, as shown here. Another option is to secure a covered button at the point where the gathers meet. (Since this creates a fixed finish, an alternative opening will be needed along the main seam of the bolster cover.)*

LEFT *Continuing the Indian theme, gauzy organzas patterned with gold were chosen for a collection of drawstring bags, cleverly converting the bolster cover design. They are perfect for holding jewellery or accessories and are simple to make. The bag is made up in the same way as the body of the Shell Drawstring Bag (see page 134), though the lining is of a contrasting fabric rather than a waterproof plastic. A channel for the drawstring can either be made along the outer edge – as for the bolster – or it can be set a little lower down the bag, thus creating a small ruffle to show the contrasting fabric when the cord or ribbon is gathered.*

CURTAINS & BLINDS

REVERSIBLE *lined* CURTAINS

The interplay of pattern and colour is what makes these curtains unique. They are completely reversible, so the main fabrics on one side could be chosen for their winter suitability, while the reverse sides are paler, transforming the room with a lighter, airier look for summer.

❧

MATERIALS

4 contrasting fabrics, preferably of similar widths, to size of curtain (see step 1 below) plus extra for ties • Basting thread • Matching sewing thread • 2.5cm (1in) heading tape to width of finished curtain

EQUIPMENT

Basic equipment (see page 138)

1 To calculate the number of widths of each fabric you need, multiply the length of your curtain pole/track by two and a half. Divide this amount by the width of your chosen fabric, and round this up to the nearest whole number. To calculate the quantity of each fabric required, multiply the length of the curtain – to sill or to floor, plus 5cm (2in) for hem allowances – by the number of fabric widths needed. If any of the fabrics have a pattern repeat, you will need to allow extra material for this. Measure the height of the pattern repeat (from the beginning of one design motif to that of the next) and add this measurement to the length of each fabric piece.

2 Now cut out all four fabrics (A, B, C and D) to the required width and length, joining up widths if required. If you are making a pair of curtains (as we have done), you will need to divide the number of fabric widths by two for each curtain. If there is an odd number of widths, cut the odd width in half lengthways and join each

half to the back or outside edge of one curtain, so that a full width is always at the front or leading edge. If you need to join fabric widths to achieve your measurement, do this with 1.5cm (⅝in) seams, sewn right sides together using ladder stitch (see Stitch Directory).

2 Now, with right sides together, lay fabrics A and B on a flat surface. Pin, baste and machine stitch 1.5cm (⅝in) seams up both sides and along the top, leaving the hem end open. Repeat this process for fabrics C and D (fig. 1). Clip the corners, then turn both sections right side out and press.

3 Lay down the A-B section with the B side uppermost. Cut a length of curtain heading tape to the width of the curtain, knot the strings tightly at one end of it and trim the ends. Pin the tape 10cm (4in) from the top of B, turning under 1cm (⅜in) at each end.

4 With the remaining fabric, make some ties, cutting a series of strips approximately 5 x 50cm (2 x 20in). Fold 1cm (⅜in) in along both long edges, press, then fold in half to make a narrow strip, turning in both ends as you do so. Press again, then machine stitch around all four sides. Fold the ties in half and place them in pairs at equal intervals along the top of fabric B, so that they slip under the heading tape; baste them and the tape in position. Lay the C-D section on top of the A-B section (so that B and C are together), aligning all three finished sides. Now machine stitch the top and bottom and the knotted end of the heading tape (following the basting line), taking in all four layers of fabric and the ties. (Avoid stitching over the loose strings, or you will not be able to gather the curtains.)

5 Now turn in hems on both A-B and C-D sections, making sure that they are the same length, and slip stitch to form invisible hems. Press. Gather the heading tape to the required width and knot the ends (fig. 2). Tidy the excess string neatly to keep it out of the way in between layers B and C. (A safety pin can be used for this.)

NOTES

❧ Choose medium- to lightweight fabrics of approximately similar weight. Silks and soft viscose velvets would work especially well.

❧ Choose pale summery colours for sides B and D, so that the curtain can be reversed for a new look during the summer months, with more muted hues on sides A and C for winter.

❧ When the curtains are reversed so that the patterned front layer is nearest the window, the light will transfuse through the layers, revealing the pattern on the other side. This is worth remembering if you want to avoid the effect; however, the subtle, patterned look can be very effective.

fig. 1

fig. 2

DO IT *differently*

The basic idea of combining layers of fabric can be adapted to make bordered cushion covers, duvets and pillowcases. These cushions opposite show a double-layered border, lined with a contrasting fabric. One side on the double border is split for the opening and finished with ties.

LEFT *A roomy laundry bag with a removable buttoned-in lining can be made using much the same principle as the curtains. Each bag is made in the same way as one of the curtains, with a deep hem turned in along the open end. A stitched channel holds some elastic in place and leaves a decorative ruffle.*

FAR RIGHT *For this double-bordered cushion, cut two squares of fabric to the full size of the finished cushion, plus a border and a seam allowance all around. Cut eight strips of contrasting fabric to the length of the main cushion piece, and to the width of the intended border, plus inner and outer seam allowances. Sew the strips to the squares, following the instructions in step 2 of Bordered*

Bed Linen (see page 80). Turn both sections right side out and press (fig. 1). Turn in the raw edges of the mitred border along one side of the cushion for the opening, and machine stitch. Place one main section on top of the other, and machine stitch from one end of the opening around three sides to the other end. Ensure that the raw edges of the border are within the stitching. Make ties (see page 83) and stitch to the opening (fig. 2).

fig. 1

fig. 2

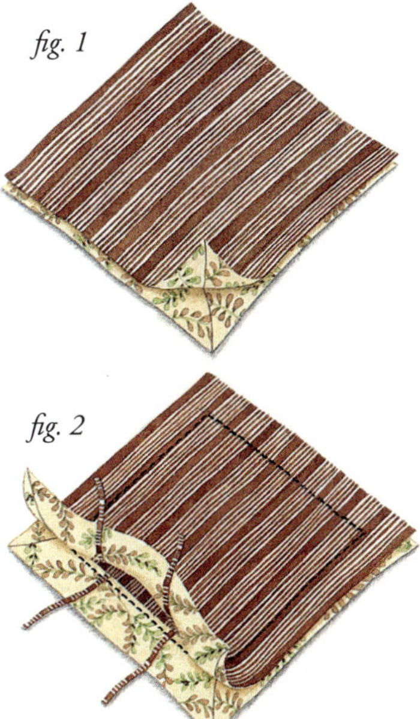

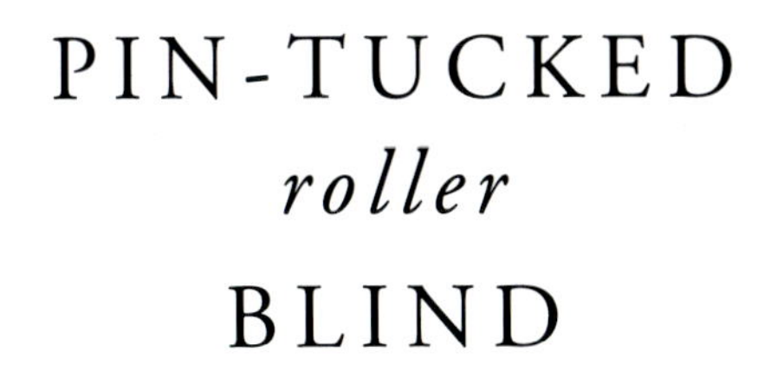

PIN-TUCKED *roller* BLIND

The plain and unfussy roller blind (shade) is the simplest of window dressings. The blinds shown here have been made up in the plainest of fabrics, which have then been subtly enhanced by a series of evenly placed horizontal pin-tucks. The fabric needs to be lightweight and slightly translucent, allowing the light to transfuse gently through in order to highlight the textural, striped effect.

❧

MATERIALS

Roller blind kit (if a kit is not available in the exact width you want, buy the next size up and cut it down to size) • Fine, lightweight fabric (enough to cover length and width of window, including seam allowances; see Notes) • Basting thread • Matching sewing thread

EQUIPMENT

Basic kit (see page 138)

1 Measure the height and width of your window, inside or outside the frame, depending on where your blind will hang. Work out at what intervals you require the stitched lines to be, and calculate how many lines will be required. Add 3mm (⅛in) per line to the final length measurement, plus 5cm (2in) for the hem and 10cm (4in) to cover the roller at the top when the blind is pulled down. Add 3cm (1¼in) side seam allowances if a fabric stiffener is not being used (see Notes).

2 If a fabric stiffener is not being used, fold both side seams under 1.5cm (⅝in), press, then another 1.5cm (⅝in) and press. Machine stitch and press again. Now, starting at the bottom edge and allowing 5cm (2in) for the hem, mark the position of your first horizontal line with pins regularly along the width, and then use these pins as a folding guideline. With wrong sides together, fold the fabric and press along this line. Remove the pins, then

machine stitch on the right side, approximately 2mm (1/16in) from the folded edge, maintaining a straight line from one end to the other (fig. 1).

3 Measure up from the pressed fold line and mark the position of the next fold; press and sew as before. Continue in this way from bottom to top (fig. 2), leaving 10cm (4in) for the top section to fix to the roller. When all your pin-tucks are complete, check the finished length of the blind and trim to size if necessary. (For ease of reference, fig. 2 shows the channel for the wooden strip stitched in place; please note, though, that this step is not taken until all the pin-tucks have been folded and machine stitched in place.)

4 Form the channel for the thin wooden strip by folding over 1cm (3/8in), pressing and then folding 4cm (1½in) and pressing again. Stitch along the first folded line, leaving the side ends open. (For a neat effect, fold your hem so that, when it is stitched, the stitching line lies just under the first pin-tuck, and is therefore invisible.) Slide in the wooden strip and overstitch the channel by hand at each end.

5 If you are using fabric stiffener, iron the fabric well, then spray the stiffener evenly all over it, and trim the sides to fit (see Notes). Attach the top edge of the fabric to the roller section, following the manufacturer's instructions. Attach the blind pull by screwing it into the exact centre on the back of the wooden strip.

NOTES

❧ Roller blind (shade) kits usually include a stiffening solution, but whether you choose to stiffen the fabric or not depends on the type of fabric used. We found a stiff, gauzy cotton that did not require stiffening. The main advantage of stiffener is that it prevents fraying, so avoiding the need to sew side seams. When heavier fabrics are used, bulky side seams prevent the roller spring mechanism from working effectively. It is still advisable to leave small side allowances, however, so that the sides can be trimmed perfectly to fit once the stitching is completed and there is no more risk of fraying.

❧ If your windows are wider than the width of the fabric, and your fabric does not have a one-way only design, run it horizontally so that the fabric joins can be disguised along pin-tucks. If this is not possible, and you have to add extra width, add an even amount of fabric to each side of the blind, matching the pattern if necessary.

❧ Experiment with unusual blind pulls. Here a curtain ring is neatly bound with a long length of fabric sewn into a fine tape. The end is hand sewn in place. An additional tie is fashioned into a decorative bow.

fig. 1

fig. 2

DO IT *differently*

The technique of pin-tucking requires a certain amount of patience, but it is well worth the effort. It can be used on many fabric-based items, such as chair covers, lampshades, tablecloths and napkins, while curtains – using the pin-tucking technique vertically – would look very special, particularly if combined with this blind.

LEFT *Here, a smart set of crisp, white bed linen has been given the same treatment to great effect. The stitching runs along the turnover end of the top sheet and down the side edges of the pillowcases. A pin-tucked bedspread to match would coordinate beautifully. The pillowcases are easy to make, following the instructions for the Felt Flower Cushions (see page 10), which sport a buttoned opening in the middle of the back of the cover. The top piece will require extra material for the pin-tucks at each end; how much will depend on how far you want the pin-tucks to extend.*

FORMAL *pleated* CURTAINS

These unusual pleated curtains are made up in a series of sculptural pleats that fall to the floor. The pleats are graduated from the top, increasing in depth until they reach the bottom, by which time the folds are substantially deeper. The curtains require a generous amount of fabric, but since they look best made up in plain fabrics – which can be bought inexpensively – the cost need not be too high.

❧

MATERIALS

Curtain fabric (see steps 1-3 below for measurements) • Basting thread • Matching sewing thread • Heading tape to finished width of curtain

EQUIPMENT

Basic kit (see page 138)

1 Decide on the number of pleats required from top to bottom of the curtain, and also on the size of the smallest pleat (at the top) and the largest pleat (at the bottom). The pleats are graduated in depth so that they become progressively larger towards the hem of the curtain. The gaps between the pleats are planned to give the required progression in size and to add up to the required total length.

When planning the curtain, it is easiest to work out the gaps before calculating the pleats, and it is simplest to choose a round number to increase by, for example, 2.5cm (1in).

Here is an example of how to plan a curtain with a finished length of 244cm (96in), with the smallest pleat starting 17.5cm (7in) from the top to allow for the heading tape:

1st gap: 7.5cm (3in)
2nd gap: 10cm (4in)
3rd gap: 12.5cm (5in)
4th gap: 15cm (6in)
and so on, increasing the gap by 2.5cm (1in) until you reach the final gap of 30cm (12in), leaving 35.5cm (14in) for the hem (see Notes).

2 Now plan the pleat sizes, making sure that each pleat hangs 2.5cm (1in) below the machine-stitched line of the previous pleat. For example, the pleat to cover the 7.5cm (3in) gap will measure 7.5cm (3in) + 2.5cm (1in) x 2 (because the pleat is double thickness) = 20cm (8in). The final gap of 30cm (12in) will be covered by a pleat of 33cm (13in), and therefore the hem – which will act as the final pleat – needs to measure 35.5cm (14in).

3 To calculate the amount of fabric required, simply add the desired length of the finished curtain to the total amount calculated for the pleats, and add 10cm (4in) for the heading and 71cm (28in) for the hem (i.e. double the hem calculation). This allows for a double hem that will be turned up and finished behind the drop of the last pleat, ensuring that the hem consists of three layers of fabric, as does the rest of the curtain. (See steps 1 and 2 of Reversible Lined Curtain [page 42] for instructions on how to calculate the width of material required, adding 15cm/6in for side hems.)

4 Press a double hem of 35.5cm (14in); pin, baste and machine stitch it in place. From the machined hem line, measure up the curtain by the depth of your bottom gap (30cm/12in) and mark it. Now from this mark measure up by the length of your bottom pleat (30cm/12in + 2.5cm/1in x 2 = 65cm/26in) and mark it. Bring the two marks together and pin and press the pleat in place. Baste and machine stitch. From this machine line measure up the next gap, which will be 2.5cm (1in) smaller, and then mark the length of the next pleat; continue as before, until you reach the top, always checking measurements carefully as you go.

5 Now turn in each side edge by 2.5cm (1in) and then 5cm (2in) and press. Hand stitch all the layers in place and press. Turn over the heading allowance of 10cm (4in) to the wrong side, press, and lie the heading tape over the raw edge. Pin and baste in place, turning under the raw edges at each end. Knot the gathering threads at one end, then machine stitch all around the tape, taking care not to sew through the gathering threads at the unknotted end.

NOTES

❧ Rather than working out your calculations only on paper, you may find it helpful to use a long length of sheeting as a mock-up on which to pin your pleats.

❧ Experiment with translucent organzas or voiles for a dramatic, structured effect.

❧ Avoid very heavyweight or thick fabrics, as the pleating will appear bulky. It is worth remembering that the finished item will effectively be three layers thick, so there is no need for lining or interlining.

fig. 1

fig. 2

DO IT *differently*

For those who feel slightly less ambitious about calculating a long stretch of pleats, or feel that the amount of fabric required is a little extravagant, the answer is to pleat just the lower section of the curtain, creating a more subtle decorative effect.

FAR LEFT *A series of pleats adds definition to this pretty, gathered lampshade inspired by old-fashioned peasant skirts. The length of fabric is seamed together, hemmed, then pleated; the top section is then folded down to achieve the right length, and a drawstring channel sewn in place a little way down from the top edge. Finally, a length of elastic is threaded through. Alternatively, use ribbon fashioned into a bow.*

LEFT *A more understated effect is achieved by pleating only the lower section of the curtain. The curtains are plainer, but still benefit from the more subtle detail, which creates weight and interest at the base of the curtains. Velvets are a good choice, the folds accentuating the depth of colour and texture.*
Cushion covers can be pleated to match. Oblong-shaped cushions with a series of vertical pleats are usually best. Once you have worked out the size and repeat of the pleats (in order to calculate the amount of fabric required for the length of the cushion), cut out the fabric accordingly and stitch the top and bottom sections together, leaving one end open for a buttoned opening. Then fold and stitch each pleat around the cushion until you reach the end. Sew buttonholes and corresponding buttons into the end pleat.

CHEQUERED *Roman* BLIND

This leafy green plaid is well suited to the tailored lines of a Roman blind (shade). The effect is an entirely well-balanced and restful window treatment. The blinds are unlined and made up in a translucent fabric that allows the linear structure of the blind to filter through. The look is light and chic, the perfect choice for summer.

❧

MATERIALS*

*Blind fabric (see steps 1 and 2 for measurements) • Matching sewing thread • 2cm (¾ in) wide touch-and-close tape to the width of the blind • Lengths of 1cm (½in) dowelling to the width of the blind • Length of 3cm x 6mm (1⅛ x ¼in) wooden strip to the width of the blind • Brass or plastic blind rings • Blind cord • Length of 2.5 x 2.5cm (1 x 1in) wooden strip to just short of the width of the blind • Screws • 3 or 4 screw eyes • Cleat or hook to secure blind cords • * but see Notes*

EQUIPMENT

In addition to the basic kit (see page 138), you will need: Staple gun • Screwdriver

1 Measure the height and width of the window, inside or outside the frame, depending on where you want your blind (shade) to hang, and decide on the number of dowelling pockets required (approximately 20cm/8in gaps between pockets are recommended). Add 9cm (3½in) to the length for hem allowances plus a further 4cm (1½in) for each dowelling pocket. Add 4cm (1½in) to the width for hem allowances.

2 Turn under a 1cm (⅜in) double hem on each side, press, baste and machine stitch. Turn down a top hem of 1cm (¼in) and then 2cm (¾in), press, baste and machine stitch. Lay the soft section of the touch-and-close tape over the top hem, and machine stitch around all four sides of the tape. Turn up a

bottom hem of 1cm (½in) and then 5cm (2in), press, baste and machine stitch, leaving the ends open.

3 Lay the blind down, wrong side up. Divide the length of the blind by the number of dowelling pockets required, always leaving a half gap at the bottom. The positioning of the pockets may be guided by the fabric. In this case the chequered design was used as a guide, with each pocket taking up one line of squares (fig. 1).
Mark the pocket positions with tailor's chalk. Fold along each line, press, then stitch 2cm (¾in) in from each fold to create 4cm (1½in) pockets. Now slide dowelling into each pocket, and the thin wooden strip into the hem. Hand stitch the ends of each pocket closed.

4 Hand stitch blind rings to each dowelling pocket – one at each end (inset 3cm/1⅛in) and one in the middle (fig. 2). If your blind is exceptionally wide, you may well require a fourth row. Now tie three lengths of blind cord (measuring approximately two times your blind length plus the width of the window) to the bottom rings and thread them up to the top.

5 Screw the remaining wooden strip to the window frame or wall, and staple the scratchy section of touch-and-close to it. Screw the metal eyes into the bottom of the wooden strip to match the positions of the rings on the blind. Place the blind on the wooden strip, and press the touch-and-close tapes together. Thread the three cords up through the eyes and, in the case of two of the cords, along the top, so that all three finish up at one side of the blind. Draw all the three strands down one side of the blind and thread through a blind pull, but do not knot them yet.

6 Using the outside cords only, level the hem along the window sill or a horizontal glazing bar. When the blind is straight, pull up the slack on the centre cord and knot the three together. Trim the cords evenly while the blind is fully down, to ensure that they are not cut too short (fig. 3). Position a cleat or hook on the wall around which to wind the cords when the blind is raised.

NOTES

❧ Instead of buying all the materials listed, buy a Roman blind kit, which will contain everything except the fabric. If you do use a kit, you may not need to use a cleat or hook to secure the cords because the kit mechanism may have an automatic clamping action.

❧ If your windows are wider than the width of the fabric, and your fabric does not have a one-way only design, run it horizontally so that the fabric joins are disguised within dowelling pockets instead of forming vertical lines.

❧ Replace an ordinary blind pull with a cluster of glassy beads that echo the colour of the blind.

fig. 1

fig. 2

fig. 3

DO IT *differently*

Quite different effects can be achieved by the clever use of fabrics. It all depends on your requirements. If you wish to disguise a dull view, but don't want to shut out the light completely, then this blind – made up partly in a translucent fabric and partly in a denser fabric – is the one for you.

FAR LEFT *A clever option that could work well in a city environment is to make up most of the blind in a dense fabric which, when dropped, neatly obliterates the view and provides some privacy; for the top section, however, use a translucent fabric, such as linen scrim, which allows the light to continue streaming through. A mitred border sewn around the edge will ensure a firm structure around the edge of the blind (see Couched Organza Tablecloths, page 74).*

LEFT *For a more nautical effect, make up the blind in a bold, striped fabric and insert eyelets at set intervals along the edge. Instead of using dowelling in ringed pockets, thread some thin rope through the eyelets; when the rope is pulled up, pleats are naturally formed. To work out where the eyelets should be positioned, fold the fabric into the required number of pleats; the eyelets will need to fall at each end of the top of each pleat. Larger screw eyes or cup hooks will be required at the top to accommodate the rope.*

BED & TABLE LINENS

APPLIQUED *denim* TABLECLOTH

A lively combination of appliqué and embroidery stitches, worked in a glorious palette of blue, decorate this hard-wearing denim tablecloth. The tablecloth features a border and bold floral motifs cut from the lighter-weight chambray fabric, which are then hand stitched in place using running stitch and a scattering of French knots. In time, the tablecloth will develop a beautiful patina as the denim gradually fades.

❧

MATERIALS

1.5m (1¾yd) of 137cm (54in) wide blue denim, to make a tablecloth approx. 127cm (50in) square • Basting thread • Matching sewing thread • 1.5m (1¾yd) of 137cm (54in) wide pale blue cotton chambray • Stranded cotton embroidery threads (floss) in various shades of blue

EQUIPMENT

Basic kit (see page 138)

1 Pre-wash both fabrics to allow for any shrinkage and loss of dye. Cut out a 137cm (54in) square of denim. Pin,baste and machine stitch a double 2.5cm (1in) hem on all four sides, mitring the corners (see Techniques).

2 To create the inset border, cut four lengths of chambray, each one measuring 8 x 112cm (3¼ x 45in), which includes a 1cm (⅜in) hem allowance all around. Turn all the edges under by 1cm (⅜in) and press; then pin and baste the strips in place so that they lie 10cm (4in) inset from the edge of the tablecloth. Using running stitch, hand stitch the borders in place with a contrasting embroidery thread (fig. 1).

3 Draw a series of petal shapes from the one shown here, or one of your own design. (The petals do not need to be identical, and any irregularities will add to the casual effect.) Six petals were used for each of the six flowers on the tablecloth shown here, but you can

choose as many petals and as many flowers as suits your design. Add on an extra 5mm (¼in) all around the petals, then cut them out.

4 Turn under the edges of each petal by 5mm (¼in), then pin and baste them in position on the tablecloth so that the flowers are scattered over the surface. Press, then, using running stitch, hand stitch them in place with contrasting embroidery threads. A variety of blues used from petal to petal creates a painterly effect.

5 Complete the tablecloth decoration with a series of loosely placed seed stitches over the background, and a scattering of French knots (see Stitch Directory) in the centre of each flower (fig. 2).

NOTES

❧ All manner of fabric combinations can be used for this kind of tablecloth. Try using floral remnants for the border and flowers placed on a chequered background or simply use the same fabric throughout, using the stitching alone for the colour contrast. Be sure to remember to pre-wash all fabrics before use, to check for shrinkage as well as dye-fastness.

❧ For a tablecloth that is going to have heavy use, it may be worth adding a lining to protect the stitching on the back. A lining of the chambray would work well, or perhaps a blue floral or check fabric for contrast. If you do decide to use a lining, follow the instructions for the tablecloth on page 85. This should be done after all the embroidery is finished. When the tablecloth is pressed right side out, an embroidered running stitch could be worked 1cm (⅝in) in from the edge all around to finish it off.

❧ Experiment with different kinds of embroidery stitches for the decoration (see Stitch Directory). Stranded embroidery threads (floss) usually comprise six strands, and you can vary the effect of your stitching by splitting the threads into different numbers of strands. Use three for medium-weight fabric, even less for fine work, but all six for heavy fabric and bold designs.

fig. 1

fig. 2

DO IT *differently*

This kind of simple appliqué work has a charmingly naive quality. It is quick and simple to perform, and ideal for decorating many items of soft furnishing. You can develop the theme by experimenting with more ambitious decorative stitching and by playing with pattern – combining florals with checks and geometric fabrics.

LEFT *To match our denim and chambray tablecloth, a tea cosy has been embellished with a jaunty teapot design and embroidered with cross stitch, daisies and French knots (see Stitch Directory). When making a tea cosy, it is advisable to make the insulating padded lining separately, so that it remains detached from the cover for easy and regular laundering. The size of the cover will therefore need to be a little larger than that of the lining, so that the one can be slipped over the other.*

ABOVE *Chambray napkins with a double mitred border (see Couched Organza Tablecloth, page 74) are embroidered with similar stitching to match. The stitches were worked carefully, catching only the top layer of the fabric, so that the back of the napkins is not marred by the reverse view of the stitching.*

COUCHED *organza* TABLECLOTH

Stiff, gauzy, silk organza has a wonderfully alluring effect, making it an unusual but lovely choice for soft furnishings. Being softly translucent, the material allows the attractive shape of the table beneath to show through, particularly when silhouetted against a light source. This tablecloth has added form and shape from a deep mitred border, with additional textural patterning in the form of a leafy motif hand couched with string.

❧

MATERIALS

Approx. 4.5m (5yd) of 115cm (45in) wide silk organza, to make a tablecloth 1.4 x 2.3m (4ft 6in x 7ft 6in) • Basting thread • Matching sewing thread • Ball of household string • Stranded cotton embroidery thread

EQUIPMENT

In addition to the basic kit (see page 138), you will need: Paper • Dark marker pen • Embroidery needle

1 Cut a 112 x 200cm (42 x 78in) piece of organza to form the main body of the cloth. Cut four strips of organza for the border, two measuring 32 x 142cm (12½in x 55in) and two measuring 32 x 232cm (12½in x 91in).

2 Mark the centre of each strip and of each side of the main piece with pins, then lay the strips on top of the main piece, right sides and raw edges together, and pin them all around the edge, matching the centres. This will leave an equal overlap at each end. Baste and machine stitch each strip in place in turn (1.5cm/⅝in from the edge), making sure that you hold the adjacent strips clear as you sew towards the corners (see Bordered Bed Linen, page 80). Stop 1.5cm (⅝in) from the edge. Trim the seams and press them towards the border.

3 Fold the border strips in half lengthways and press, then unfold

(fig. 1). To mitre the border corners, follow the border mitring instructions in the Techniques, but stitch diagonally from the inner corner only as far as the fold line – not right to the outside edge. Trim the seam edges, then refold the border along the fold line. Tuck in the unstitched sections of the seam to form a neat mitre at one corner, and mark where the stitching will go with tailor's chalk. Unfold the border to trim the edges (fig. 2), then refold and slip stitch the seam. Repeat for the other three corners. Now turn under the edge of the border all around so that it lies along the seam to the main square. Pin, baste and slip stitch it in position (see Stitch Directory).

4 Draw your motif on a sheet of paper, using a dark marker pen; then, when the pen lines are dry, place the translucent organza cloth over the top. With a white tailor's pencil (sharpened to a fine point) gently mark your design on the tablecloth.

5 Now simply lay a length of household string along the traced design and, using the embroidery needle and thread, couch it in place (see Stitch Directory), tucking under any loose ends and sewing them neatly.

NOTES

❧ When sewing organza, it is essential that the seams are trimmed evenly and neatly, as untidy work will show through this translucent fabric.

❧ The design to be couched should be as fluid as possible, requiring the minimum of loose ends, which can look messy.

❧ When ironing the finished piece, place the tablecloth string-side down on a few layers of towels laid flat on the ironing board. It is impossible to iron the cloth successfully directly on the ironing board because the surface will be too bumpy.

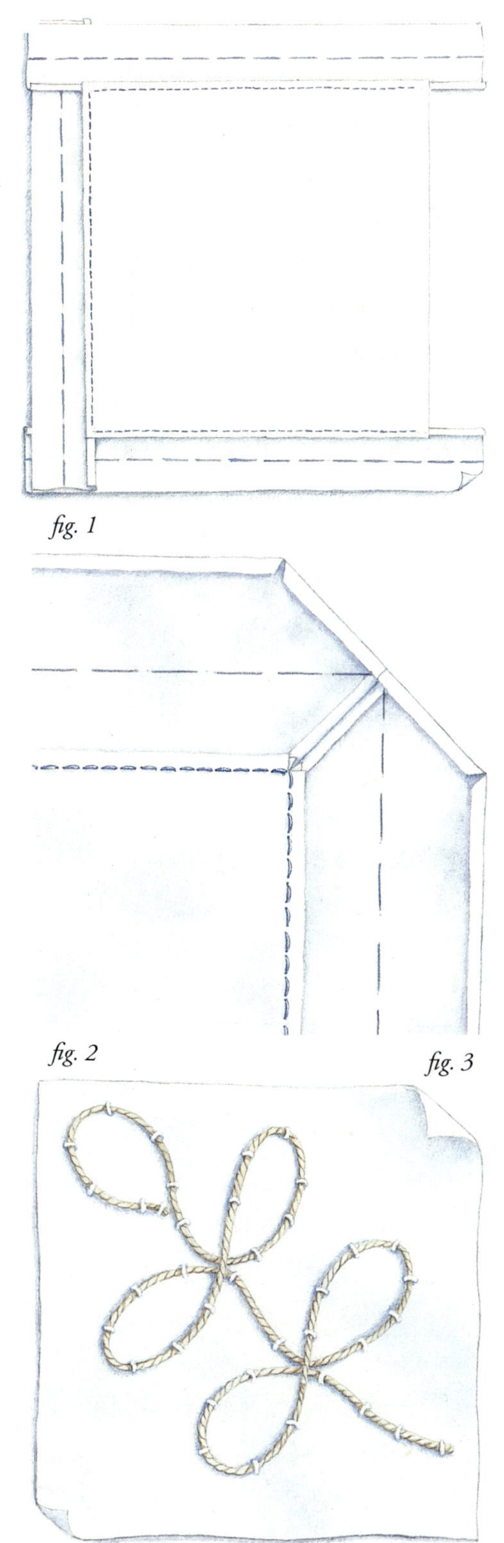

fig. 1

fig. 2

fig. 3

DO IT *differently*

The technique of couching can be used to decorate almost anything. It can be worked into motifs as the sole decoration, or used to finish the edges of appliqué or to emphasize the edge of a bold fabric design. Coloured and decorative cords, heavy threads, twines and string can all be used. A gold cord stitched on to velvet looks rich and sumptuous.

FAR LEFT *Inexpensive white cotton piping cord, available in lots of different weights, is easy to work with, and can be home dyed to match a particular fabric. The throw features a decorative border that is stitched down, except for the loops, which remain free. Instead of couching the cord in place, a more discreet slip stitch was used.*

LEFT *Piping cord has also been used to decorate this cushion, where it has been worked into a monogram and used as a loopy trim to border the edge. Other items that could benefit from this simple form of decoration include blinds (shades), curtains, bed linen and lampshades.*

BORDERED *bed* LINEN

Making your own bed linen in fine-quality cottons or linens is very satisfying and economical. The choice of fabrics that are wide enough for making double-sized bed linen is usually very restricted. By adding a border around the edge of a double duvet cover, however, average-width fabrics can be combined to make up the full width required.

❧

MATERIALS

Two contrasting fabrics, each with a minimum width of 90cm (36in) – about 2.5m (2¾yd) of fabric A and about 8m (8¾yd) of fabric B • Basting thread • Matching sewing thread

EQUIPMENT

Basic kit (see page 138)

1 Take fabric A and cut it into two equal squares, using the full width of the fabric. Take fabric B and mark on it eight equal pieces for the borders, each 200cm (78in) long, and each wide enough so that when placed either side of A the combined width will be 200cm (78in). Add 3cm (1⅛in) to both measurements for seam allowances. For the inner flap to tuck the duvet into, cut a further strip from fabric B, measuring 203 x 36cm (80 x 14in) by 36cm (14in) wide. For ties, cut 10 strips measuring 36 x 7.5cm (14 x 3in) from fabric A or B.

2 Fold the border lengths in half to locate the centre points and mark these with pins, then unfold the borders; do the same to all four sides of each A square. Pin the borders to the squares, right sides together; the border strips will overlap, and you will have to hold the adjoining strips out of the way as you baste and stitch each one in turn, ending the stitching 1.5cm (⅝in) from each corner (fig. 1). Mitre the border at all eight corners (see Techniques).

3 Now turn in 5mm (¼in) along one long edge of the inner flap, press, then fold over a further 1cm (⅜in). Press again, and machine stitch to make a neat top edge. Place the flap at the bottom of one side of the quilt cover, raw edges and right sides together. Baste, then machine stitch the seam. Press the flap to the wrong side of the cover, and pin and baste the sides in place (fig. 2). Turn up a double hem on the bottom edge of the other bordered square, as above, and baste.

4 With wrong sides facing, and the hemmed edge of one square corresponding with the flap edge of the other, place the two halves of the cover together, and sew French seams (see Techniques) around the edges, leaving a bottom central opening of about 150cm (60in). Sew reinforcing stitches at each side of the opening. Turn right side out.

5 To make the ties, fold 1.5cm (⅝in) to the wrong side along both edges of each strip. Then fold each strip in half, wrong sides together, and stitch across the ends and along the sides. Pin the ties to both inside edges of the opening, spacing them equally and so that they correspond as pairs from one side to the other. Machine stitch them in place (fig. 3).

6 The pillowcases shown here have been made with a flat, mitred-edge border, Oxford style. A simpler method, however, would be to use the same technique as for the duvet. In this way, the pillowcases would still have a contrasting border, but it would be part of the body of the case and not a flat edge. The ties that feature on the duvet cover would obviously not be needed.

NOTES

❧ A contrasting fabric border, neatly mitred, can be used to give a fresh look to everyday household items, such as towels, plain blankets or even plain, unlined curtains.

❧ Experiment with check fabrics with a contrasting stripe for the bordered edge. (It is important to ensure that the stripes match up at each corresponding corner of the cover.)

❧ If you have decided to use a narrow-width plain fabric for the whole duvet, try embellishing the inner and outer bordered edge seam with a pattern of decorative embroidery stitches or a braid. The same braid can also be used for the ties. All-white bed linen would look great highlighted with a colour that co-ordinates with other furnishings.

fig. 1

fig. 2

fig. 3

DO IT *differently*

This beautiful, reversible tablecloth – in a combination of contrasting checks, stripes and florals – is made in exactly the same way as a single layer of the duvet cover.

FAR LEFT AND LEFT *Another simple use of the basic mitring technique is the tablecloth shown here. This time a floral fabric is juxtaposed with a stripe and then lined with a check. The combination of the three is usually a successful formula. The tablecloth sports a mitred edge on one side, and is then simply lined with a square of fabric. The two layers would be stitched around three sides, right sides together, and then turned right sides out, and the gap neatly hand stitched. Alternatively, the edge could be bound with a deep red tape or a strip made up in one of the fabrics.*

QUILTED *crib* COVER

A hand-stitched crib quilt is an attractive and useful additional layer to help keep a young baby snug and warm. Opt for two contrasting fabrics so that the quilt is reversible, and a medium- to lightweight wadding (batting). The quilting is hand worked using little running stitches in a simple criss-cross design, with a basic border around the edge. A neat ruffle adds an endearing finishing touch.

❧

MATERIALS

Approx. 50cm (20in) of 137cm (54in) wide fabric (A) • Approx. 1m (39in) of 137cm (54in) wide fabric (B) • 50cm (20in) of washable medium- or lightweight wadding (batting)• Matching sewing thread • Basting thread • Quilting thread

EQUIPMENT

In addition to the basic kit (see page 138), you will need: Quilting frame (optional) • Quilting foot (if quilting by machine)

fig. 1

1 Cut a rectangle from fabrics A and B to the required size of the finished quilt (ours measured 105 x 80cm/42 x 32in), adding a 2cm (¾in) seam allowance all around. Cut a layer of wadding (batting) to the same size but with no added on seam allowance. If your fabric is plain, you will need to

measure and mark the quilting lines at this stage, using a tailor's pencil and a ruler (fig. 1). Mark them on the right side of fabric A. (If your fabric is checked, like ours, then the simplest method is to use the printed lines as guidelines for the quilting.)

2 Cut a strip of fabric B long enough to go twice around the edge of the quilt, and 5cm (2in) wide. Cut this strip on the cross (diagonal) if you wish, for a contrast effect. Fold the strip in half lengthways, and sew the ends together. Machine stitch two parallel rows of stitches right along the raw edges of this strip, using large stitches. Pull both cotton threads to gather the strip into a ruffle to fit the edge. Adjust the gathers evenly.

3 Lay fabric B right side up on a flat surface. Lay the ruffle on top so that the raw edges are together, then pin, baste and machine stitch in place, 1.5cm (⅝in) in from the edge.
Press fabrics A and B thoroughly, making sure that the ruffle is pressed to the outside. Lay fabric B wrong side up and place the wadding (batting) on top, joining widths if necessary with a large herringbone stitch (see Stitch Directory). Now lay fabric A, right side up, on top (fig. 2). Pin and baste all three layers in place. Start your stitching from the centre and work outwards to the edge; this will prevent the fabrics from slipping and puckering (fig. 3).

4 Make sure that both fabric layers are smooth. Now you are ready to stitch. Use a quilting thread, which is thicker and stronger than standard sewing thread, and a simple running stitch. If your wadding (batting) is more than a thin layer, use a quilting frame, working the quilt section by section, to ensure that your stitches are vertical. Start with the middle section, stitching in parallel lines to create a criss-cross pattern. Sew each line in the opposite direction to the last in order to prevent the fabric from slipping or puckering. Now complete the border from the inner edge to the outer edge.
Finally, turn under the edge of fabric A all around, and slip stitch it to fabric B along the stitching line of the ruffle.

NOTES

❧ Using a contrasting coloured thread for the quilting is particularly effective if the quilt is made in a plain fabric.

❧ If you would prefer to quilt by machine rather than by hand, use a quilting foot, quilting thread and a large stitch. Ensure that the tension of the stitch is correct, and machine stitch each row in the opposite direction to prevent the fabric from slipping. If using a machine, quilt the top layer of fabric to the wadding (batting) and then to sew the lining on to the back.

❧ Our design here is one of the simplest traditional patterns worked on old quilts. A more complicated design would be worthwhile on a plain fabric.

fig. 2

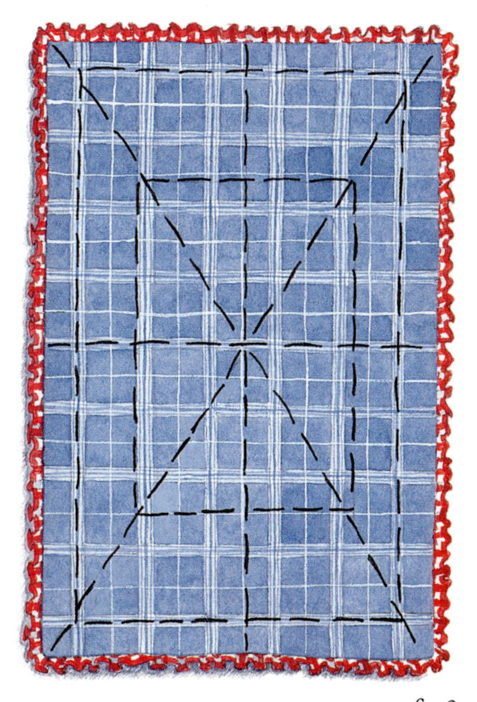

fig. 3

DO IT *differently*

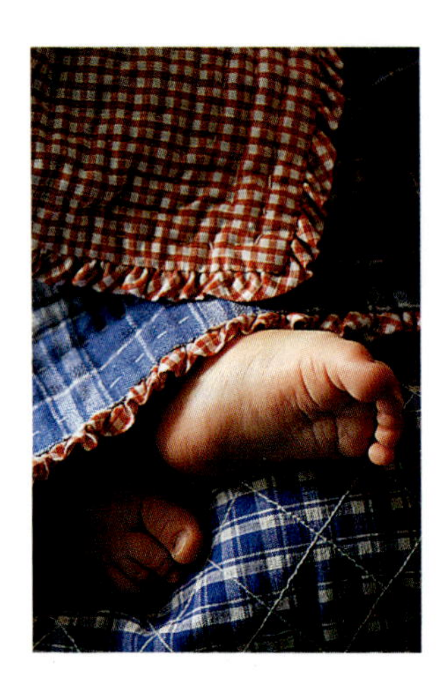

Quilted curtains are a great idea for a young child's room. They have excellent insulation properties to help keep draughts at bay, and they are relatively simple to make (although you need lots of patience – and quilting thread – for the stitching).

LEFT *Quilted curtains are a wonderful, textural option for a bedroom. A traditional Provençal design was chosen here as it featured a small motif printed on a diagonal repeat that lends itself to the quilting method. To hand quilt both curtains would have been too time consuming, so the quilting was done on the sewing machine, using a large stitch and special quilting thread. The main fabric was quilted to the wadding (batting), then the lining was applied afterwards to avoid puckering. Each curtain was finished off around the edge with binding, and a simple gathering tape was applied at the top.*

ABOVE *This simple understated crib quilt made in an antique cream linen has been worked in a contrasting white linen thread. Working on a small item like this is a great way to start quilting because the size of the job is not too daunting.*

CANOPIES & SCREENS

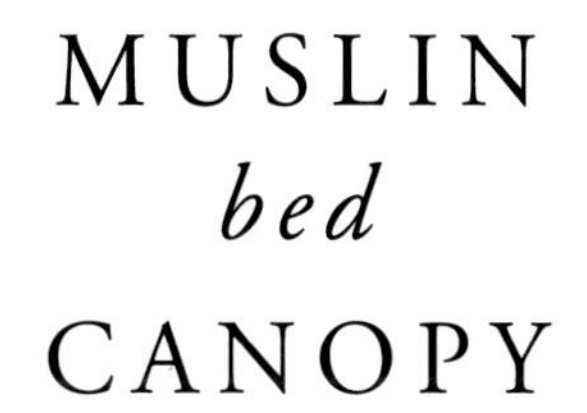

MUSLIN *bed* CANOPY

Swathes of fine butter muslin make up this simple bed canopy which romantically graces an old iron bed. The canopy is principally decorative but would work admirably as a mosquito net. Large amounts of fabric are required to create such a luxurious effect, so an inexpensive fabric such as muslin is a good choice. The canopy boasts a minimum of structure, so it is light and will simply hang from a hook secured to the ceiling.

MATERIALS

13m (14yd) of muslin, approx. 130cm (51in) wide • Basting thread • Matching sewing thread • Circle of plastic-coated garden wire (sold in a coil) measuring approx. 45cm (18in) in diameter • Roll of adhesive tape (masking or insulating)

EQUIPMENT

Basic kit (see page 138)

1 Cut five lengths of muslin about 253cm (100in) long. This includes an extra 30cm (12in) for the hem, and 12.5cm (5in) for the heading. (These measurements were correct for our room; experiment to see what will be right for you.) Pin, baste then machine stitch the five lengths together at the sides, using the French seam technique (see Techniques). Press. The remaining ends, which will form the opening of the canopy, can be left as they are, with the selvages forming the edge, or they can be turned in and stitched.

2 Fold over the top 7.5cm (3in) of the fabric to the wrong side and press. Now fold the top 4.5cm (1¾in) of the folded edge back to the right side, creating four layers of fabric, and press. The 4.5cm (1¾in) flap on the right side will constitute the final ruffle. Pin, baste and machine stitch 5mm (¼in) from the top edge, securing all four layers of fabric. Press. This line of stitching also forms the top of the pocket that will contain the wire circle.

To complete the pocket, turn under the bottom 1cm (⅜in) of the 3cm (1¼in) section of fabric (now reduced to 2.5cm/1in by the top seam line). Pin and baste it to the main fabric, ensuring that you hold the ruffle on the reverse side out of the way to prevent it from becoming entangled. When this is done, machine stitch the hem. You will now have a finished pocket of 1.5cm (⅝in) (fig. 1). Press.

3 To complete the hem, fold over 15cm (6in), and then fold this over again to make a double hem, and press. Baste, then machine stitch along the top edge of the hem (see Notes).

4 Thread a single section of plastic-covered wire through the pocket until the canopy is tightly gathered (fig. 2). Secure the two ends where they join with a length of strong adhesive tape. Pull the gathers back over the join so that both ends meet.

5 Cut four sections of fabric to make the ties, each measuring 100 x 7.5cm (39 x 3in). The length will depend on how large you require the final bows to be. Fold each tie in three lengthways and press, leaving a triple-thick tube of 2.5cm (1in) in width. Tuck under the raw long edge and both ends, and then pin, baste and machine stitch all around. Now hand stitch the ties in place, equidistantly spaced around the inside of the canopy.

6 Pull up the opposite ties to an equal length,and knot them together in pairs, one above the other. Tie the ends in generous bows.

NOTES

❧ The amount of fabric required depends on the height at which the canopy is hung. One way to economize is to lower the height of the head by increasing the length of the tie. If you are using muslin, which is inexpensive, this may not be a problem; but for a more expensive fabric, such as the one used for the canopy shown on page 98, this tip is worth bearing in mind.

❧ The depth of the hem is optional, but these measurements will ensure a weighty hem that will drape nicely.

❧ Trim the muslin canopy with fabric that co-ordinates with the bed linen, valance or curtains. A deep, double strip could border the hem, while a narrow strip trims the edge of the ruffle. For a demure finish add a little bow in the contrasting fabric at the top opening .

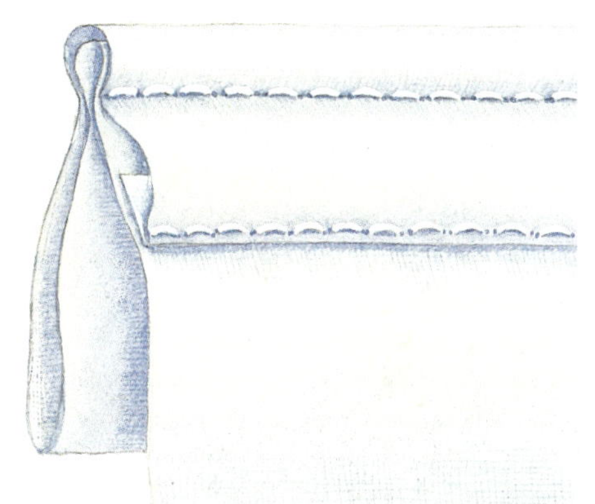

fig. 1

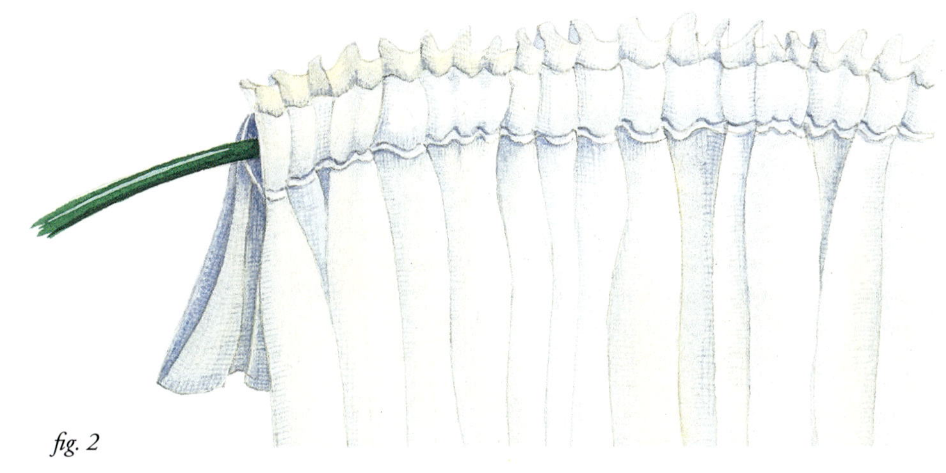

fig. 2

DO IT *differently*

One of the easiest ways of creating a different look is to choose one of the ready-dyed muslins. Bright yellow, orange, pink or red could inspire a bedroom with a romantic Eastern feel. Alternatively, try dyeing lengths of fabric to the shade you want, using the dye before you begin to make up the canopy to ensure that it is cast evenly.

FAR LEFT *The same canopy can also be made up in a patterned furnishing fabric, resulting in a completely different look. A young child would adore this pretty pink chequered version scattered with flowers. The bed is positioned against the wall, and the canopy suspended directly over the middle, allowing the fabric to drape over each end of the bed.*
The effect has a more permanent look, emulating the grand old Empire-style coronets and bed hangings.
The canopy has been lined with butter muslin (the fabric used for the project canopy), which effectively masks the wrong side of the fabric and creates a soft, tent-link interior.
To make this canopy, simply follow the instructions for the muslin version, replacing the fine muslin with a light- or medium-weight fabric. How much fabric you require will depend on the weight of the fabric chosen; however, you will need a minimum of three widths to stretch around a single bed. The more widths you join together, the fuller the effect. You will find that there is less potential with a thicker fabric for a full gather, unless the size of the wire circle is increased to accommodate the extra bulk of the fabric.

LEFT *An extra tie fashioned into a bow over the canopy opening completes the dainty look and echoes the bows above.*

SUMMER *garden* CANOPY

Nothing could be more straightforward than a length of tough canvas, hemmed and punctured with eyelets to create an instant garden canopy. Strung up from the strong boughs of a tree, or some other permanent structure, with perhaps an additional stake or two pegged to the ground, it provides a temporary garden shelter offering protection from bright sunlight or light rainfall.

❧

MATERIALS

4m (4½yd) of 137cm (54in) wide heavyweight cotton/polyester canvas (available from specialist shops such as sailmakers) • Basting thread • Matching heavyweight sewing thread • Large-size brass eyelet kit • Lengths of lightweight rope or twine • Tent pegs • Wooden stakes

EQUIPMENT

In addition to the basic kit (see page 138), you will need: Hammer

1 Cut the 4m (4½yd) length of canvas in half widthways, then sew the two pieces wrong sides together along two of the selvages, using a flat fell seam (see Techniques). This method results in a strong, flat seam that can be seen on the right side of the fabric. Now turn under double 2.5cm (1in) hems along all four sides, overlapping the hems at the corners to make six layers, then pin, baste and machine stitch in place. Press.

2 Following the manufacturer's instructions, hammer two brass eyelets into each corner – one on either side of the exact corner to avoid the six-layer thickness. Eyelet kits contain the die needed for this process.

3 Thread rope or twine through the eyelets and then tie the ends to the strong branch(es) of a tree, where possible. Other corners can be tied to the top of wooden stakes and then tent pegged to the ground for stability.

NOTES

❧ Your canopy can be made as large as you like. If yours is much larger than the one shown here, it may require extra eyelets along the length of the canopy for additional support.

❧ If you have no other permanent structure, metal or wooden stakes can be erected at all four corners; these are then pegged to the ground.

❧ This canopy is easily transportable, and, if a waterproof canvas is used, can double up as a groundsheet for a picnic.

DO IT *differently*

A heavy-duty canvas is the obvious choice for a tough and hard-wearing canopy, but for less regular use – and particularly just for a special occasion – furnishing-weight cottons will do. An option is to line decorative fabrics with a light canvas to create a strong double layer, with the added interest of contrasting or matching colours.

FAR LEFT *Here we have a cheerful floral print teamed with bright orange, which together add a flamboyant blaze of colour to an otherwise dull patio area beside the house. Two corner eyelets are simply hitched over a couple of hooks secured to the outside wall. The remaining corners are then secured to a couple of wooden stakes and pegged to the ground.*

LEFT *The canopy is enhanced with a double-sided flap that hangs along all four sides. An ambitious variation – more suited to a plain or striped fabric – would be to trim the canopy with a scalloped flap (see Scallop-edged Napkin, page 132, for instructions on making a scalloped edging).*

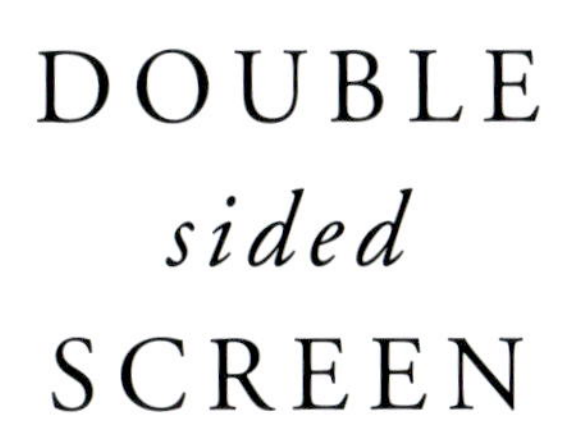

DOUBLE *sided* SCREEN

Screens are infinitely versatile in their use. They make great room dividers and are useful for concealing untidy corners; alternatively, if placed in front of windows or glazed doors, they can replace blinds or curtains as a form of screening. The flat surface provides a good opportunity to display a pictorial fabric. When the screen is reversed to reveal a matching stripe, the decorative emphasis of the room will instantly change.

MATERIALS

Wooden frame or solid wooden screen • Equal amounts of main and contrasting fabric for front and back of screen, and also of interlining (if lightweight fabric is used) • Braid to go around all sides of each panel • Fabric glue • 6 brass screen hinges and screws (for a four-panelled screen)

EQUIPMENT

In addition to the basic kit (see page 138), you will need: Staple gun • Screwdriver

1 If your screen is hinged together, or you are re-covering an old one, strip off any old fabric, staples and hinges.

2 Measure the length and width of each panel, adding on just over half the depth of the frame to each measurement to allow for stapling. Cut out a piece of both the main and contrasting fabrics for each panel. Also cut two pieces of interlining per panel (if needed), with no stapling allowance. If your fabric has a pattern repeat, be sure that each consecutive panel matches up.

3 Lay the first panel on a flat surface and stretch the interlining (if used) across the frame, stapling it to the front edge of the screen. Start at the top or bottom, beginning at the centre and working out to each corner, then proceed down the sides of the panel, ensuring that an even tension is created. Trim the excess interlining neatly (fig. 1). Repeat on the reverse side.

4 Now staple the contrasting fabric to the screen, using the same technique but stapling to the side of the panel rather than to the front edge. Fold down the corners and staple in place for a neat finish, then trim any excess fabric (fig. 2). Turn the panel over and staple the main fabric to the other side in the same way, but turning under a small hem as you go so that the fabric lies approximately along the middle of the frame. Proceed with each panel in this way, checking that patterns are correctly repeated, and mark the panels 1, 2, 3 and 4 with a tailor's pencil.

5 Now you are ready to glue the braid along the side edges, to cover the lines of staples. Follow the glue manufacturer's instructions, and start from the bottom edge, working all around (fig. 3). Finish off by turning in the raw edge and glueing it down on top of the starting raw edge to bond it and so prevent any fraying.

6 Finally, position panels 1 and 2 right sides together, and screw in screen hinges one-third of the way from the top and one-third of the way from the bottom. If the screen is exceptionally tall or heavy, three hinges should be used instead of two. Now place panels 2 and 3 wrong sides together and, lastly, panels 3 and 4 right sides together, to ensure that the screen will stand in a zigzag position; attach hinges as before.

NOTES

❧ Ensure that the braid is no wider than the width of the screen's side edges. It is also important that the braid or trimming is not a great deal lighter in weight than the fabric used on the screen, or you will find that it will not cover up the stapled seams adequately. You will find a wide selection of decorative braids in most stores that sell furnishing fabrics.

❧ If you would prefer an alternative to using braid, choose decorative brass-headed upholstery tacks, and hammer them closely together in a line all the way around. A good furnishing fabric store will usually stock a selection in various sizes and finishes.

❧ Experiment with various different shaped headings. A gentle curve, a scallop or a Gothic arch are the simplest alternatives. The heading can be cut out of chipboard (particle board) using a jigsaw. Make sure that the board is of the same depth as the screen itself. Once cut, it can be glued to the top edge of the screen and covered with both fabrics and the decorative braid, along with the rest of the panel.

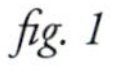

fig. 1

fig. 2

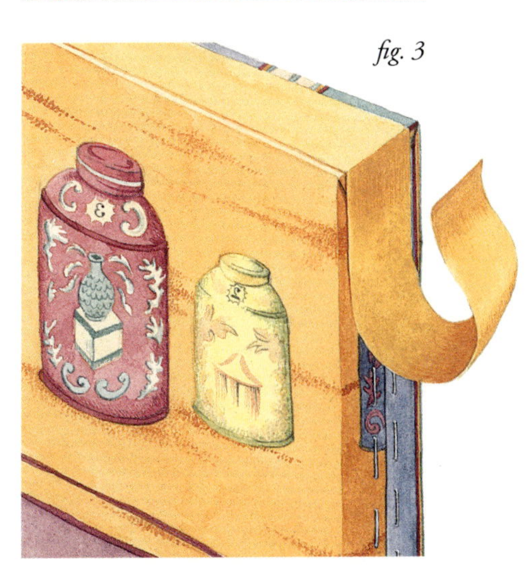

fig. 3

DO IT *differently*

The simplest screen boasts little structural detail, which means that the decorative element is left to the fabric chosen to form the panels. The panels of a screen are like a blank canvas awaiting your choice of fabric and decorative detail.

LEFT *This purple and cream covered screen has been transformed into a notice-board. Lengths of cream tape have been stapled diagonally to the sides of the screen at equal distances, then buttons were sewn in place at the cross-over points. It is important to do this before covering the reverse side of the screen in order to make the sewing easier.*

ABOVE *Experimenting with unusual fabrics can create some interesting surprises. A screen covered with translucent organza allows a very subtle screening from bright sunlight or an unlovely view. Tiny wired paper violets were sewn on to the screen using see-through thread, and the sides were finished in a matching braid.*

STRIPY *beach* TENT

This portable beach tent is quick to erect and provides shelter from sun, wind and sand, as well as privacy for changing on the beach. It has a main central pole and is secured in position by a series of guy ropes that are pegged into the ground. Two more poles support the doorway, which acts as a canopy when open. Sand and white stripes were chosen so that the tent blended in with the natural landscape.

❧

MATERIALS

Approx. 9m (9¾yd) strong canvas • Basting thread • Strong sewing thread • Heavy-weight stiffening material • Large metal eyelet kit • 4 x 90cm (36in) lengths of 2cm (¾in) diameter dowelling • 1 central wooden pole 2.3m (7ft 6in) long • 2 wooden poles 1.8m (6ft) long • Tent pegs • 20m (21¾yd) twine or lightweight rope

EQUIPMENT

In addition to the basic kit (see page 138), you will need: Hammer

fig. 1

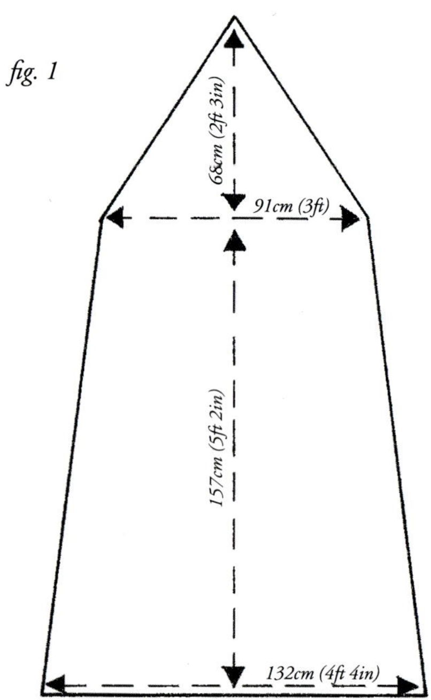

1 Cut out four of the sections shown in fig. 1, and add seam allowances as follows: 3cm (1⅛in) for side and roof seams, except for those on the door and on either side of it, which need 5cm (2in), and 16cm (6½in) to allow for deep double hems. Cut four strips (87 x 9cm/34½ x 3½in) for the dowelling

pockets. Mark each section carefully with a tailor's pencil: 'door', 'right', 'left' and 'back'.

2 Fold the fabric at each roof base and press. Take each dowelling pocket and fold in 1cm (⅜in) at each end; baste, then machine stitch. Fold each pocket, wrong sides together, in half lengthways, and press; fold in 1cm (⅜in) edges along both long sides and press. Pin and baste together. Now pin a pocket along the pressed line on the wrong side of each main section (leaving a 3cm/1⅛in gap at each end). Baste and then machine stitch in place (fig. 2).

3 Turn in 1cm (⅜in) and then 4cm (1½in) on the door section from the base of the roof down the two sides. Pin, baste and machine stitch. Do the same to the opening edge of the left and right sections. Press.

4 With wrong sides together, pin the back to the left and right sections, allowing 3cm (1⅛in) seams from the apex of the roof all the way down the two side seams. Then pin together the two remaining roof sections. Stitch using a strong flat fell seam (see Techniques), trimming the seams very slightly as you approach the apex so that they can lie flat. You may find this easier by hand. Ensure that the hole at the apex is no larger than an eyelet. Finally, turn up double 8cm (3¼in) hems; pin, baste and machine stitch.

5 To make the eight tags, cut out 16 sections 10 x 14cm (4 x 5½in), rounding off one end of each. Cut a piece of stiffening to fit one section, and baste it to the wrong side. Now, with right sides together, pin, baste and machine stitch both layers of fabric (and the stiffening) around both sides and the rounded end, leaving the top square end unstitched. Turn the tag right side out and press. Topstitch 1cm (⅜in) from the edge. Fold the raw-edged end over 1cm (⅜in) and then 2cm (¾in) and press. Repeat for the other seven tags, then hammer in metal eyelets in the rounded ends (fig. 3).

6 Machine stitch the tags at each corner of the base of the roof, stitching back and forth a few times. Hammer in metal eyelets in the positions shown in fig. 4 and another large eyelet through the roof apex. Insert the dowelling in the pockets; hand stitch the ends closed, then hand stitch each pocket end to the next one.

7 Place the central pole in the ground and erect the tent. Attach twine or rope to the tags and bottom eyelets, and secure with tent pegs.

NOTES

❧ For a more robust tent, build a more structured framework and choose a heavier-weight waterproof canvas.

❧ Smaller eyelets fixed on and beside the door allow it to be laced closed.

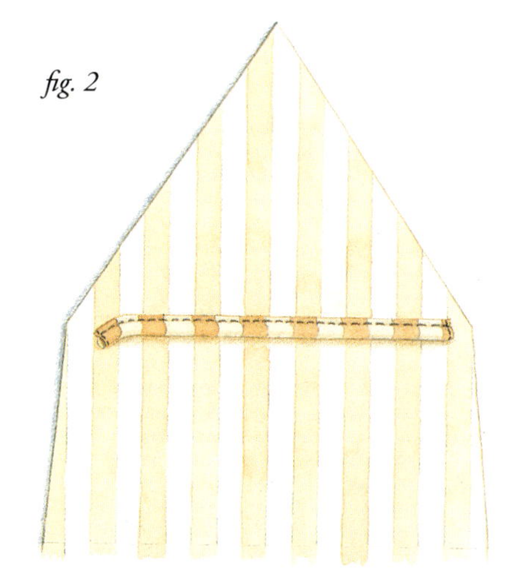

fig. 2

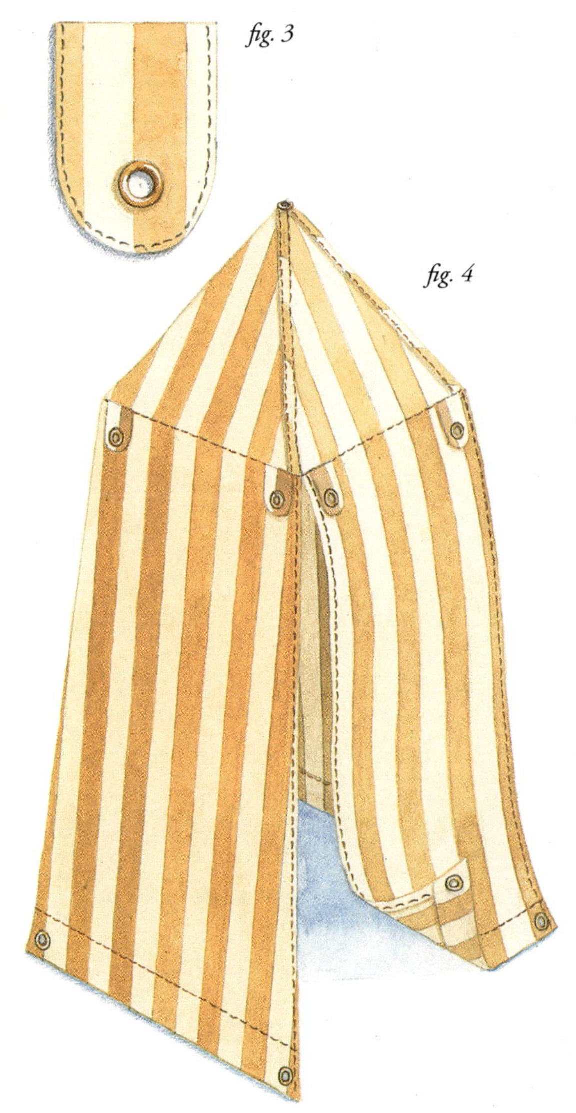

fig. 3

fig. 4

DO IT *differently*

The basic design of the beach tent converts very neatly into a tented wardrobe or shelf cover. Dressing up shelves in this manner is a great way of reviving dull shelving almost anywhere in the home. Choose cool, natural linen for a bathroom or a lively, stripy, contemporary fabric for a bedroom.

FAR LEFT *Here we show the tent made up to the dimensions of a set of basic wooden shelves to create a fashionable and inexpensive alternative to a bedroom cupboard. To create the tented roof section, you will need to construct a basic roof structure from chipboard (particle board) consisting of two triangles slotted together crosswise, set diagonally across the top of the shelving and screwed in place on the top. Otherwise opt for a flat-topped design, which could feature a fancy scalloped or zigzagged pelmet (valance) around the top edge. (This edging would be stitched to a flat top section and then placed over the top of the main shelving cover like a lid.)*

LEFT *The cupboard shown here is frequently used, and so ties have been positioned on the inside of the doors and the outside of the front corner side seams for ease of opening. The two doors are then simply drawn back and tied in position. Another alternative would be to have a series of ties arranged evenly down each side of the opening and tied together down the middle.*

ACCESSORIES

hotos
Letters

ACCESSORIES *and* STORAGE

The smaller-scale projects provided in this chapter include an appliquéd lampshade with couched design variation, ideas for storage (a lined work basket and a fabric-covered box), a damask ironing-board cover, a beautiful quilted Moses basket, a generously sized napkin with decorative scalloped edging and, finally, a drawstring bag decorated with shells and raffia work.

❧

APPLIQUED AND COUCHED LAMPSHADES

MATERIALS

Medium-weight cardboard • Linen • White stranded cotton embroidery thread • Spray glue • Fabric glue • Masking tape 1.5cm (⅝in) wide

EQUIPMENT

In addition to the basic kit (see page 138), you will need: Old lampshade • Pencil • Craft knife • Small bulldog clips

1 Separate the old shade from its frame, and cut along the join. Place the old shade on the cardboard and mark the shape, adding a 1.5cm (⅝in) overlap at one end. Cut out, using a craft knife. Place the cardboard template on the cross of the linen and mark the shape, allowing a 1.5cm (⅝in) turning allowance along the top and bottom edges and along one end (fig. 1).

2 Cut flowers and leaves from the remaining linen, arrange them on the linen shade, then slip stitch them in place with the raw edges turned under. Embroider the final details on the appliquéd shapes. Lightly spray the cardboard shade with glue; lay the right side of the linen shade on a table, and place the cardboard on top. Trim the edges to 6mm (¼in) and clip. Apply fabric glue to the underside of the turning allowances and stick them to the cardboard (fig. 2). Leave to dry.

3 Bend the shade into shape, overlapping the ends, and check that it will fit the metal fittings perfectly, using clips at top and bottom to hold the shade in place. Apply some fabric glue to the underside of the finished (i.e. turned) end of the shade and glue the two ends together, overlapping them by 1.5cm (⅝in). Hold the ends in place until the glue is completely dry.

4 Now slip in the fittings at top and bottom and use masking tape to secure them in position around the inside edges of the shade. Cover the raw fabric edges with tape, clipping along both edges so that it lies flat (fig. 3).

fig. 1

fig. 2

fig. 3

LEFT *This elegant conical shade has a subtle decoration of gently curving tendrils on its textured, hessian-like surface. The design is formed from household string, couched in place with tiny bar stitches (see Stitch Directory and also Couched Organza Tablecloth, page 74).*

LINED WORK BASKET

MATERIALS

Basket • Fabric (see step 1 to calculate quantity) • Thin wadding(batting) to go around the side of the basket, over the base and in the divider • Thick linen thread

EQUIPMENT

Basic kit (see page 138)

1 Measure the basket. Mark on the fabric two main sections (A), both measuring the sides of the basket x the height, one top base section (B), the length (including divider) x the width, and one lower base section (C), the length x the width (see fig. 1). Add a 1.5cm (⅝in) seam allowance all around, then cut out the pieces.

Cut one piece of wadding (batting) to fit A, one to fit C, and one to fit the divider, with no seam allowances. Cut 5cm (2in) wide binding (on the cross) long enough to go around the top and bottom of the liner, three sides of the divider, and the joining seam of A, plus enough to form four ties 41cm (16in) long and two ties 20cm (8in) long.

2 Pin and baste the wadding (batting) to the wrong side of one of the A sections. Pin and baste the other A on top of the wadding (batting), wrong sides together.

Fold B in half, mark the height of the basket on both sides of the fold, and fold the fabric back on itself at these points (see fig. 2). Pin and baste the thin strip of wadding (batting) to the wrong side of the flap, and the other piece to the wrong side of C. Reverse the flap and assemble the base as shown in fig. 3. Pin and baste all around.

3 Mark a criss-cross pattern on one side of each section, using a ruler and pins or tailor's chalk. Quilt by hand, using a thick linen thread and even running stitches (see Stitch Directory).

4 Pin, baste and machine stitch the side seam of A; trim the seam and press. Pin A to B (right sides together), easing the fabric around the corners. Make sure that the side seam of A aligns with one end of the dividing flap. Baste and machine stitch. Trim and press.

5 Take enough of the binding strip to go around C and along the side seam of A. Fold in 1cm (⅜in) along both raw edges and press, then pin, baste and hand stitch over the seams. Pin the remaining binding strip to the inner top edge of A, raw edges together. Baste and machine stitch, 1cm (⅜in) from the top. Fold over the strip, turning in another 1cm (⅜in), on to the outer side. Pin, baste and slip stitch. Finally, work running stitch along the binding, taking in all the layers.

6 Trim the vertical sides of the divider so that it does not buckle when pulled taut at both sides, then repeat the binding process along its sides. Add another strip along the top edge, extending 20cm (8in) to each side to act as single ties. Finish as before.

7 For each tie, fold in 1cm (⅜in) along both raw edges of binding strip, then fold the strip in half. Pin, baste and machine stitch along the open long edges, and finish with hand stitching. Fold them in half and sew the long ones on at the top corners and the short ones halfway along each side.

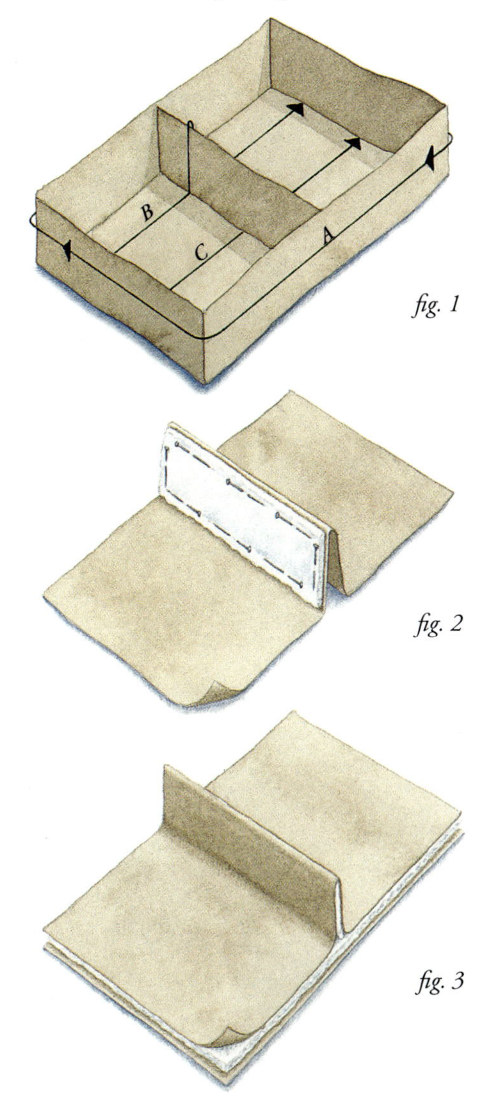

fig. 1

fig. 2

fig. 3

FABRIC-COVERED BOX

Plain boxes can quickly be converted into a good-looking filing system for stowing away old photographs, letters and other important bits and pieces that need a home. Covered boxes are a great solution for the home office environment, where it helps if such necessities can be smart and decorative – and even colour coded. These handsome, spotty boxes sport hand-stitched labels, which give them a quirky, homespun touch.

MATERIALS

Lidded box • Fabric to cover box and lid • Scraps of contrasting fabric for labels • Embroidery thread • Basting thread • Matching sewing thread • Fabric glue • Contrasting fabric for lining, if required

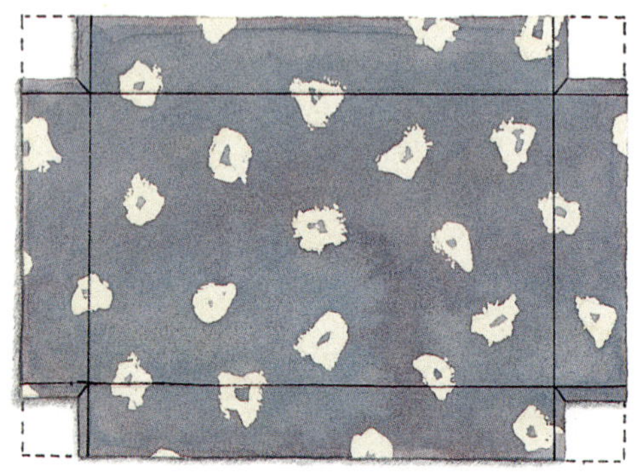

fig. 1

fig. 2

EQUIPMENT

In addition to the basic kit (see page 138), you will need: Fabric glue

1 Remove the lid, and place the box on the wrong side of the fabric. Mark all four sides of the base on the fabric with a tailor's pencil (going right to the corners, see below). Measure the depth of the box and add 3cm (1⅛in) for the overlap on to the inside of the box, and extend the marked rectangle or square by this amount on all four sides. Cut out along the marked lines. Measure diagonally outwards from each base point corner by 1cm (⅜in); then, from this point, draw straight lines out to either side, to form a right angle. Cut out the square that has now been formed at each corner, and clip diagonally from the corner point to the corner of the base.

2 Place the corner seams right sides together, then pin, baste and stitch along the marked lines. Press the seams open, then turn the fabric box right side out. Now place the box inside the fabric box and check for a perfect fit, adjusting the seams if necessary.
Remove the box and apply a thin layer of fabric glue to its base, then replace it in the fabric and press down firmly. Glue along all four sides of the fabric where they overlap the box, and press them firmly and smoothly over the top and down on to the inside of the box to form a neat finish.

3 To cut the fabric to line the box, if desired, follow the same instructions but measure just to the top of the box. Once the seams are sewn, do not invert the fabric cover, as you did for the outside. Turn down the top 1.5cm (⅝in) and press. Glue the base and sides of the inside of the box, and place the lining inside; the turned edge should cover the raw edge of the outside fabric by 1.5cm (⅝in).

4 Repeat these instructions for the box lid, but before sewing or glueing the fabric, apply any labels you want. Cut out labels from contrast fabric, adding a small turning allowance all around. Turn under the edges and press. Mark lightly the word or motif you wish to apply, and embroider using a simple stem stitch (see Stitch Directory). Now pin the label to the middle of one of the lid sides, and secure it to the main fabric by a series of French knots (see Stitch Directory).

Paper
Photos
Letters

DAMASK IRONING-BOARD COVER

Ironing-board covers are usually made of rather unattractive fabrics, and inevitably soon wear out or become unpleasantly stained. So try giving yours a new lease of life by covering it in a favourite fabric, preferably cotton or linen which are hard-wearing. The cover is softly padded and is simply secured over the board by pulling and tying the drawstrings tightly underneath the board. The cover is therefore easily removable and can be laundered when necessary to maintain a crisp surface.

MATERIALS

Damask or other fabric to cover board • Lining fabric to cover board • Medium-weight wadding (batting) to cover board • Approx. 3m (118in) of 12mm (½in) tape • Basting thread • Matching sewing thread

EQUIPMENT

In addition to the basic kit (see page 138), you will need: Sheet of paper • Safety pin

1 Lay the paper on top of the ironing board, and trace around the outer edge as far as the metal plate. Cut around the outline to create a template.

2 Place the template on the main fabric and add 10cm (4in) all around the sides and the curved end, and 2.5cm (1in) along the straight end. Cut out. Repeat with the lining fabric and also the wadding (batting).

3 Pin and baste the wadding (batting) to the wrong side of the main fabric. Machine stitch 3cm (1¼in) in from the edge along the sides and the curved end, stopping 2.5cm (1in) in from the straight edge. Trim off excess wadding (batting) close to the stitching line, and also 2.5cm (1in) in from the straight end.

4 Place the main and lining sections right sides together; pin, baste and machine stitch around the main outer edge, 1cm (⅜in) in from the raw edge. Trim and clip around the curved edges. Turn separate 2.5cm (1in) hems to the wrong side of both fabrics at the straight end; press and baste in place (fig. 1). Turn right side out and press.

5 Baste, then machine stitch, the layers together, following the stitching line that joins the wadding (batting) to the main fabric. This will leave a channel of 2cm (¾in) between the two stitching lines. Slip stitch together both turned-in hems at the straight end, stopping short of the drawstring channel on either side (see Stitch Directory). Now attach one end of the drawstring tape to a safety pin, close the pin, then thread it through the channel, leaving even amounts of tape at both ends (fig.2).

Lay the finished cover on top of the ironing board, pull the tape up tightly so that the cover fits snugly, and secure the ends underneath the board.

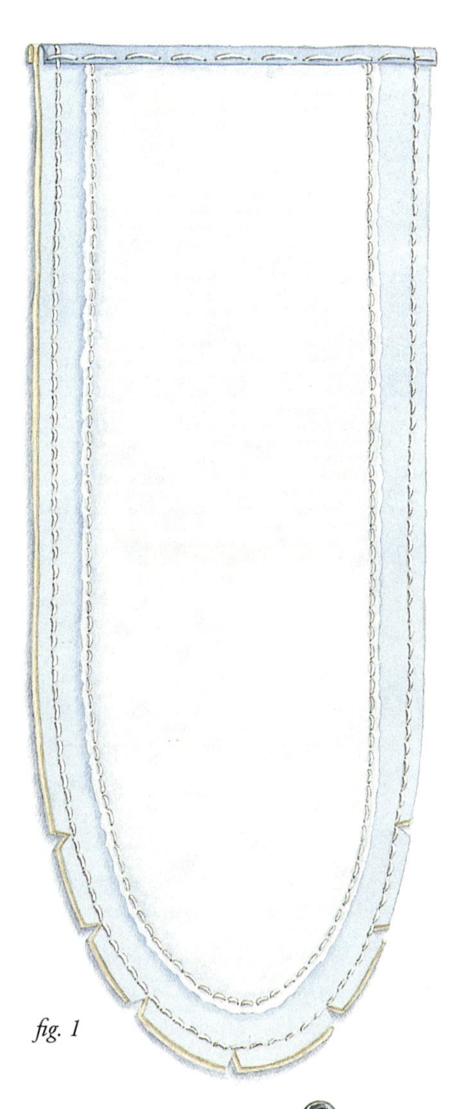

fig. 1

fig. 2

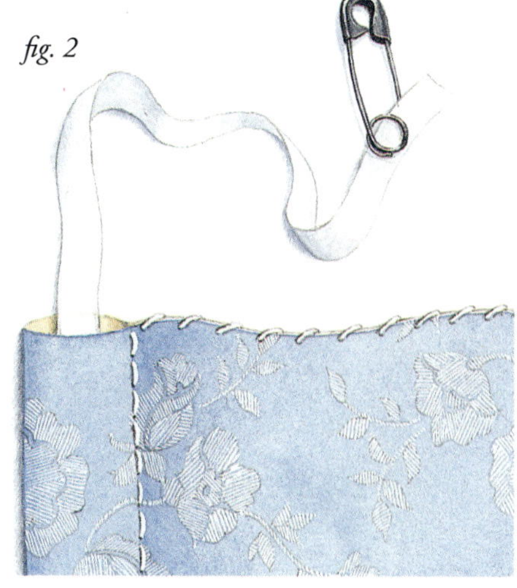

QUILTED MOSES BASKET

MATERIALS

Moses basket • Main fabric for inside of liner (see step 1 for quantity) • Lining fabric for outside (see step 1 for quantity) • Wadding (batting) • Basting thread • Matching sewing thread

EQUIPMENT

In addition to the basic kit (see page 138), you will need: Masking tape

1 Measure the circumference of the top edge of the basket and also its depth. Use these two measurements to mark a rectangle on both the main and lining fabrics, adding a 1.5cm (⅝in) seam allowance all around. Mark a similar rectangle on the wadding (batting), but with no seam allowance. Cut out all three rectangles. Make a template of the basket base, adding a seam allowance as before. Use this template to mark and cut out two base sections (fabric and lining). Cut a 6cm (2½in) strip of binding to go around the edges of the liner, plus enough for some 41cm (16in) ties. (We used 12.)

2 Place the main fabric piece inside the basket, right side towards the basket. Adjust the fabric to fit the basket by inserting darts at the curved ends (see fig. 1). Baste the darts, check that the liner now fits the basket well, then machine stitch. Repeat this process for the lining piece.

3 Lay the main fabric piece right side up, and, using a ruler, mark a criss-cross pattern with pins or tailor's chalk. The lines should be about 6cm (2½in) apart. Concentrate on the sides and each end rather than the darted areas. Lay the wadding (batting) on the wrong side of this section and baste in place. Now turn the fabric over and machine quilt along the marked lines, sewing each line in the opposite direction (to avoid any danger of puckering), and also down each dart line. With the ends of the quilted fabric right sides together, pin, baste and machine stitch the side seam (fig. 2).
Finally, seam the lining section, then fit it to the quilted section, wrong sides together. Ensure that the edges are aligned, then pin and baste in place.

4 Place the base sections wrong sides together, then pin, baste and machine stitch all around. Pin the base section to the main section, main fabrics together; baste and machine stitch in place. Trim and clip. Press.
Place the liner in the basket and mark where the ties should lie. Make up each tie by turning in both raw edges and ends by 1.5cm (⅝in) and pressing, then folding each strip in half and pressing. Pin, baste and machine stitch all around. Fold in half to form two ties, and hand stitch to the marked places on the liner.

5 Baste a length of binding strip all around the top edge of the liner, right side to right side of main fabric. Machine stitch 1.5cm (⅝in) in from the top. Press. Fold over the strip to the lining side, turning in another 1.5cm (⅝in). Pin and slip stitch.
Place the remaining strip around the lining side of the main section, to align with the bottom edge, and machine stitch it along the seamline. Press the strip over on to the base, then turn in the other side and slip stitch (fig. 3).

fig. 1

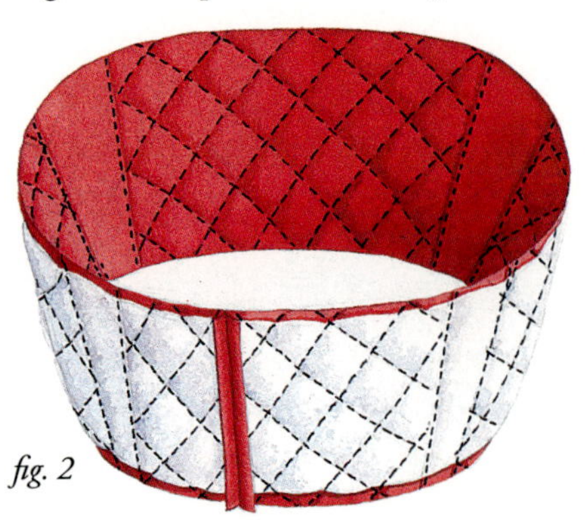
fig. 2

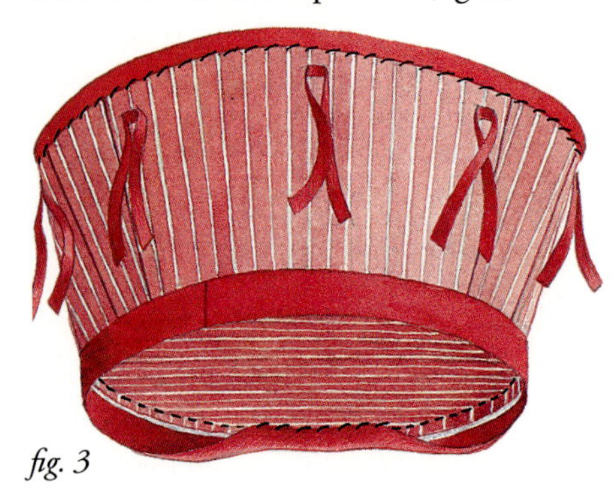
fig. 3

SCALLOP-EDGED NAPKIN

A contrast-patterned, scalloped edging transforms these simple cotton napkins into an extremely pretty dining accessory. To complete the look, try making a tablecloth with a matching scalloped edge on a larger scale.

MATERIALS

Contrasting fabric for border (see step 1 for calculations) • Approx. 45cm (18in) square main fabric • Basting thread • Matching sewing thread

TOOLS

In addition to the basic kit (see page 138), you will need: Marker pen • Circular template

1 First cut eight strips from the contrasting fabric, 45cm (18in) long, plus enough fabric for an extra scallop at each end. The width should be the diameter of the circular template plus approximately 4cm (1½in).

2 Pin two strips right sides together, making sure that any fabric pattern (in this case stripes) aligns. Wth the ruler and the marker pen, draw a line along the middle of one side of the double strip. Now use your template to mark the scallops, beginning and ending with a ¾ scallop, and using the middle line as a guideline. Trim the fabric 1cm (⅜in) away from the line marking the scallop edges, and then cut notches around each curve and up into the join of each scallop (fig. 1). Pin and then machine stitch the scallops, carefully following the marker lines. Trim to about 5mm (¼in). Turn right side out and press. Repeat for the remaining three borders.

3 Now join the border strips by mitring the scallops together. Align two finished borders at right angles (see mitring borders in Techniques), folding both ¾ scallops back in half to create a diagonal line (fig. 2). Match up patterned stripes, if necessary. Press both fold lines. Trim excess fabric to leave 1cm (⅜in) to tuck inside each scallop to hide the raw edges, leaving aligned, folded edges on both sides. Slip stitch along both sides.
Mitre the remaining three corners to create a scalloped border.

4 Now measure the inside of the border and add on 3cm (1¼in) to both the width and the length. Cut out the main fabric square to these dimensions, and slide it in between the two open lengths of each border. Turn under the raw edges of the border by approximately 1.5cm (⅝in) and pin them to the main fabric on both sides. Baste, then slip stitch in place on both sides (fig. 3). Press.

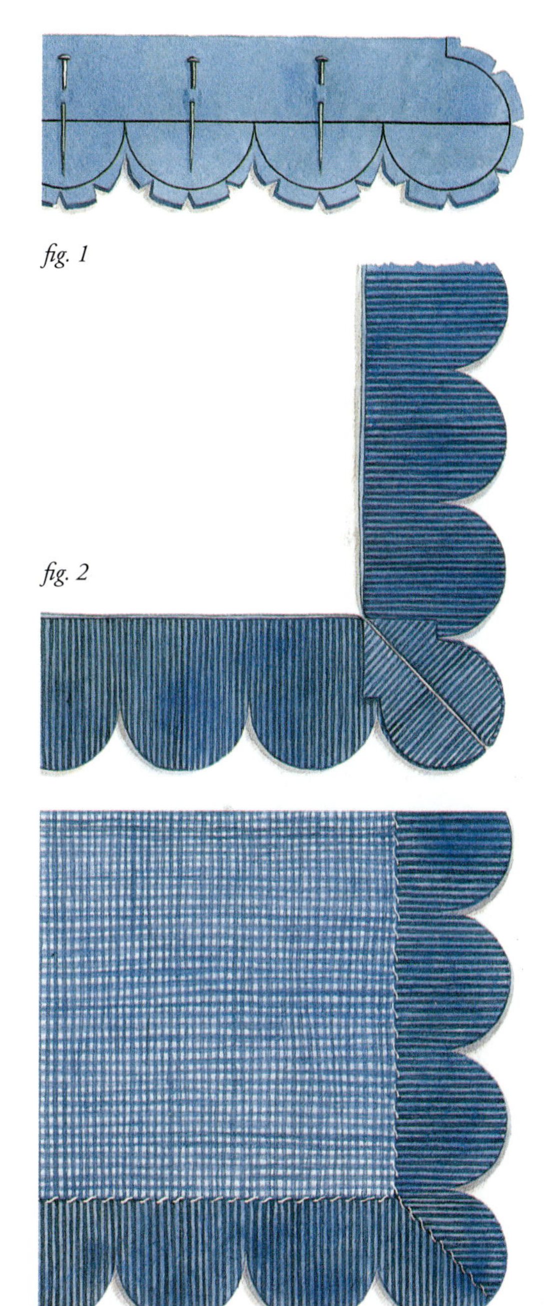

fig. 1

fig. 2

fig. 3

SHELL DRAWSTRING BAG

MATERIALS

70cm (28in) of main fabric (137cm/54in wide) • 60cm (24in) of plastic lining (137cm/ 54in wide) • Basting thread • Matching sewing thread • Approx. 50 shells • Coloured raffia • Hardboard cut to 16 x 9cm (6½ x 3½in) oval • Fabric glue

EQUIPMENT

In addition to the basic kit (see page 138), you will need: Electric or hand drill • Fine drill bits

1 From both the main and lining fabrics cut out a bag section (66 x 20cm/26 x 8in), an oval base (16 x 9cm/6½ x 3½in) and a top band (66 x 15cm/26 x 6in), adding a 1.5cm (⅝in) seam allowance all around. Also cut a length of main fabric 120 x 2.5cm (48 x 1in) for the loops and two lengths of 90 x 2.5cm (36 x 1in) for the drawstrings. These will be threaded through the V loops at the end.

2 With right sides together, sew the side seam of the main fabric bag section to form a cylinder. Press. Pin the base section to the cylinder, right sides together, taking up the excess fabric by forming pleats around the curved ends of the base. Fold over the top 1.5cm (⅝in) of the cylinder to the wrong side, press and baste (fig. 1). Repeat with the lining fabric. Machine stitch the fabric and lining to their bases.

3 With right sides together, sew the side seam of the top band and press. Fold it in half to form a band 9cm (3½in) wide, press, turn in 1.5cm (⅝in) along both long edges, and press again.

4 Take the 120 x 2.5cm (48 x 1in) length and fold in both long edges to meet in the middle, then fold it in half to form a strip 6mm (¼in) wide. Cut into twelve pieces, each 10cm (4in) long. Now place at equal intervals around the top edge of the bag, doubled up into V shapes, and baste in place.

5 Drill holes in the centre of each shell, and sew them to the main body of the bag and along one side of the top band. Use lengths of raffia to decorate around each shell with a few stitches and French knots (fig. 2) (see Stitch Directory for some examples).

6 Check that the hardboard oval fits within the seamline at the base of the bag, then apply a thin layer of fabric glue to one side of it and stick it in place. Place the lining bag in the fabric bag, wrong sides together, aligning side seams and top edges. Pin, baste and machine stitch, sandwiching the ends of the V loops. Take the top band and align its side seam with that of the bag. Slip the top ends of the V loops between the two turned-in edges. Pin, baste and machine stitch (fig. 3). Press.

7 Finally, make up both 90 x 2.5cm (36 x 1in) lengths into strips as before – though this time sewing across the ends too – to make two drawstrings.

fig. 1

fig. 2

fig. 3

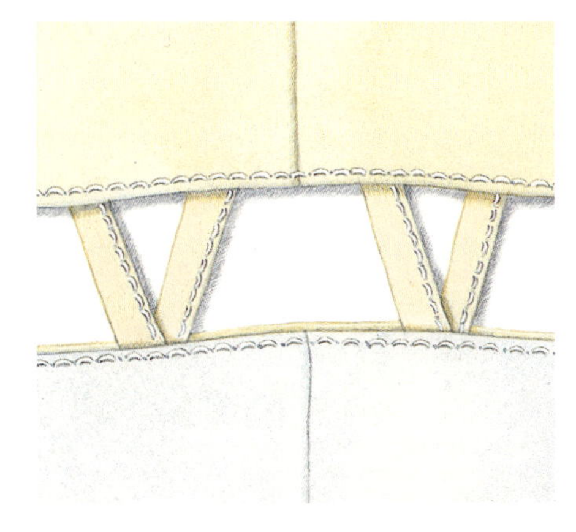

STITCH *directory &* TECHNIQUES

The advanced needleworker will need no reminding of the simple stitches and techniques used in these projects, but the beginner may find the following illustrations and explanations helpful.

BASIC SEWING KIT

These items form a basic set of sewing equipment, and many of the projects in this book require no additional tools or equipment. When extra items are needed, they are listed for that particular project.

Dressmaking scissors
Hard straight edge (such as a steel ruler)
Iron and ironing board
Pencil
Pins and needles
Sewing machine
Tailor's pencil

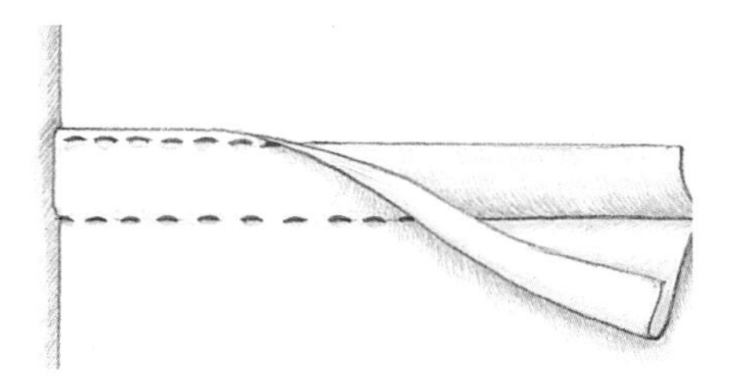

FLAT FELL SEAM

A strong, self-finishing seam, commonly used for soft furnishing items that will endure a lot of wear.
Place the two pieces of fabric right sides together and sew a plain seam. Now trim one side of the seam allowance and fold the other side over to cover both raw edges. Stitch along the fold line.

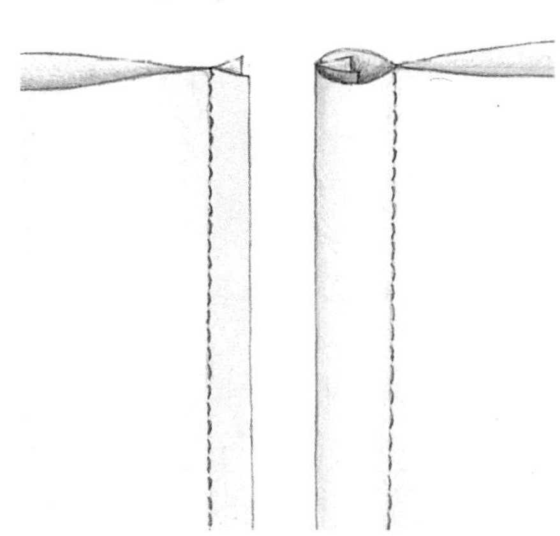

FRENCH SEAM

A two-step, self-finishing seam for fabrics that might otherwise fray at the edges. Sewing starts with the wrong sides of the fabric together.
Start with wrong sides together, and sew a plain seam. Press the seam open, then turn the fabric so that the right sides are together. Sew a second seamline to enclose the raw edges. Press this seam open and turn the fabric right sides out again.

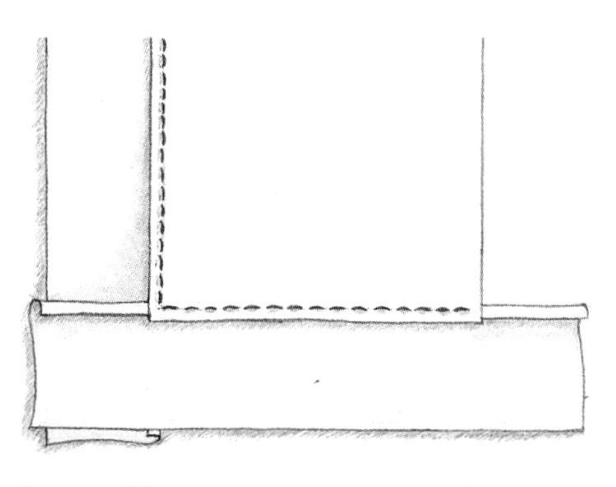

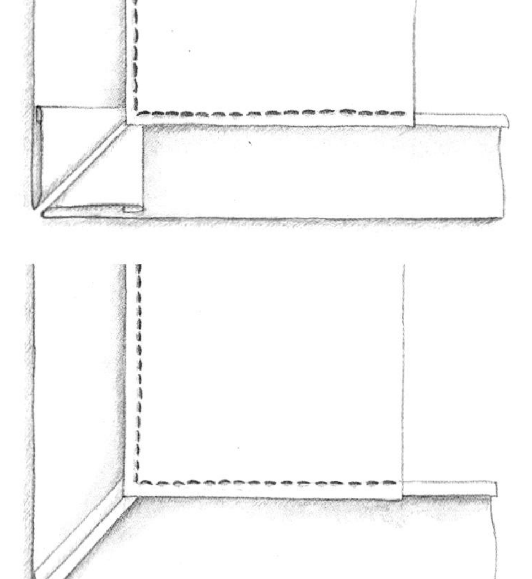

MITRED BORDER

Attach the border strips to the main fabric, sewing up to the seam allowance at each corner.
Place the right sides of two border strips together, and crease from the stitched corner to the outside edge, creating a triangular flap of each fabric. Check that this is a true 45 degree angle to the border edge with a set square (draftsmans triangle). Stitch from the inner corner to the outer corner, then trim the seam edges.

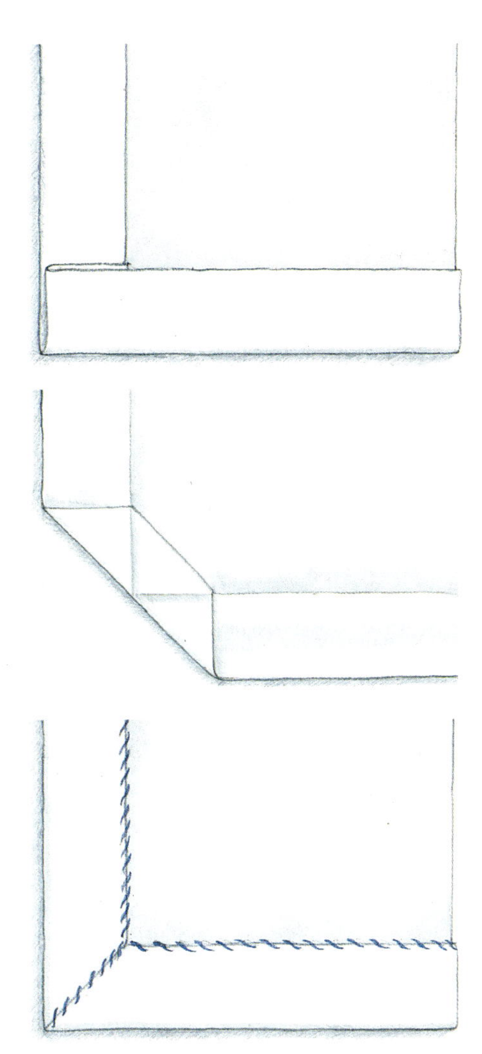

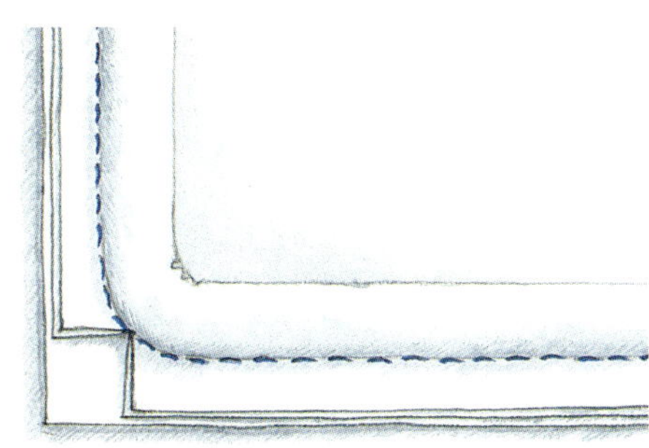

PIPING

To join strips of fabric from which to cut piping lengths, put the strips at a 90 degree angle, right sides together, and machine stitch along the join.
To cover the piping cord, fold the fabric strip around the cord, right side out. Pin, baste and machine stitch close to the cord, using a zipper or piping foot on the machine. Where lengths of covered cord need to be joined, fold back the fabric, and trim the cord ends so that they meet end to end. Unfold the fabric so that it covers the abutted ends, turn under a 5mm (¼in) hem, and stitch over the join.
To apply piping to a seam, lay the piping on the right side of one piece of fabric, raw edges together. Pin and baste. Machine stitch as close to the stitching line as possible, using a zipper or piping foot. Clip the seam allowance on the piping to ease the fit on any corners. Place the other section of fabric on top, right sides together, and pin, baste, then machine stitch, following the existing stitching line.

MITRED CORNER

*Turn in side and bottom hems and press. Open out the hems, and *fold in the corner of the fabric at the point where the two pressed lines cross, checking that the pressed lines on the triangle align with those on the fabric. Cut off the corner. Turn in the hems again to form a neat join; slip stitch the edges and the hems. For a double mitred corner, turn up double side and bottom hems, unfold one layer, then proceed from*.*

TURK'S HEAD KNOT

Follow the illustrations carefully, using ribbon or a thin strip of fabric, to form this decorative knot. Pull the ribbon or fabric gently at the final stage.

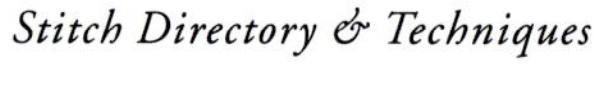

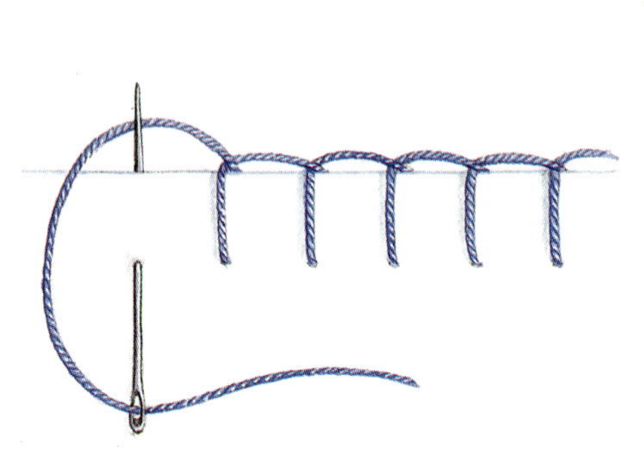

BLANKET STITCH

Use this stitch to finish raw edges or as a form of decoration.

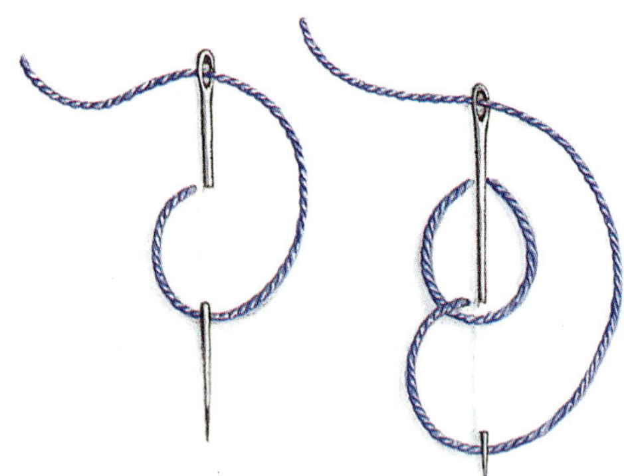

CHAIN STITCH

One of the most simple embroidery stitches, formed by looping the thread around consecutive vertical stitches to form interlinking loops.

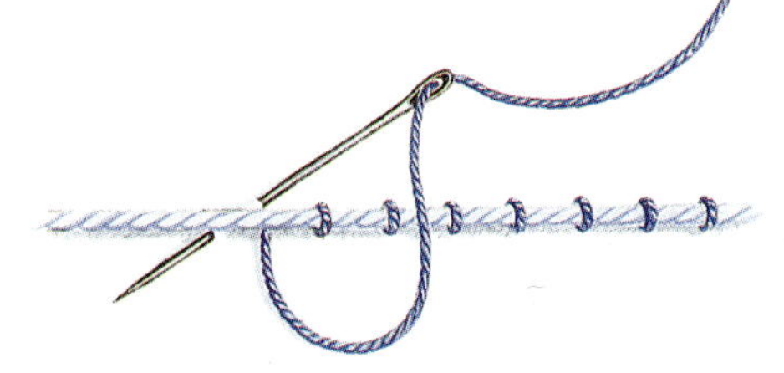

COUCHING

A form of fabric decoration involving a series of bar stitches worked in a fine thread that hold down a length of cord or string on top of the fabric.

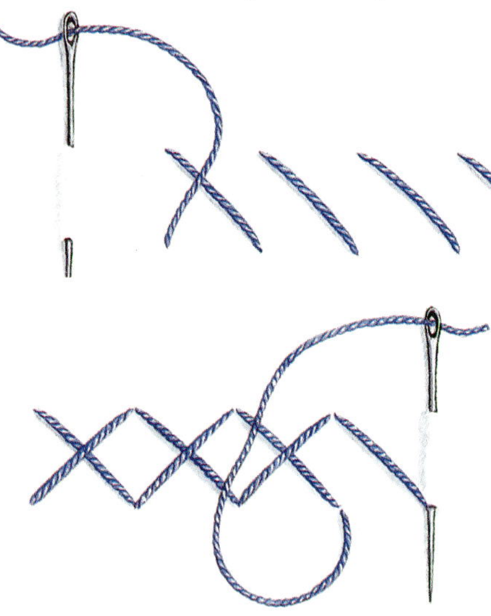

CROSS STITCH

Work half the crosses from right to left, then work back from left to right, adding the finishing stitches.

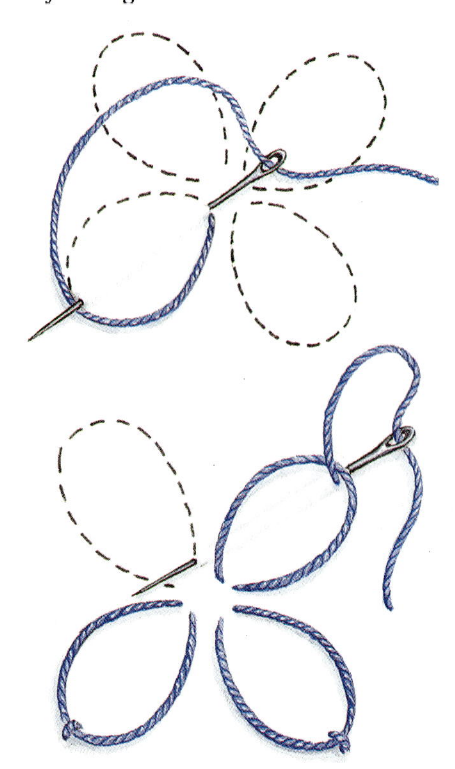

DAISY STITCH

In this variation on chain stitch, small tying stitches keep the daisy petals in place.

FEATHER STITCH

Single feather stitches are worked alternately to left and right to achieve the feather effect.

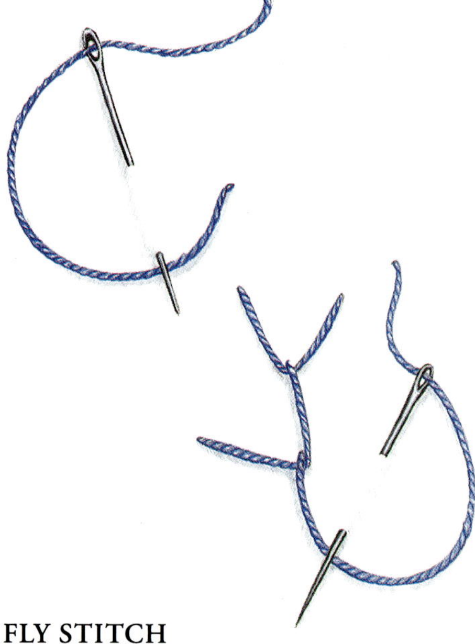

FLY STITCH

Diagonal stitches worked to the centre are held in place by vertical tying stitches.

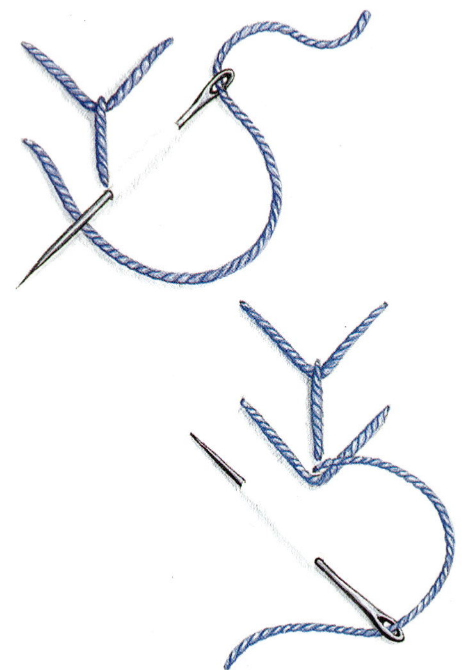

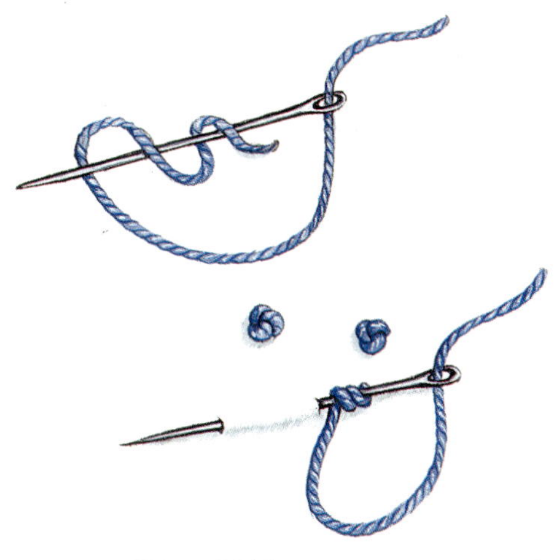

FRENCH KNOT

This raised stitch is worked by winding the needle twice through the thread, then inserting the needle close to the point where it came out.

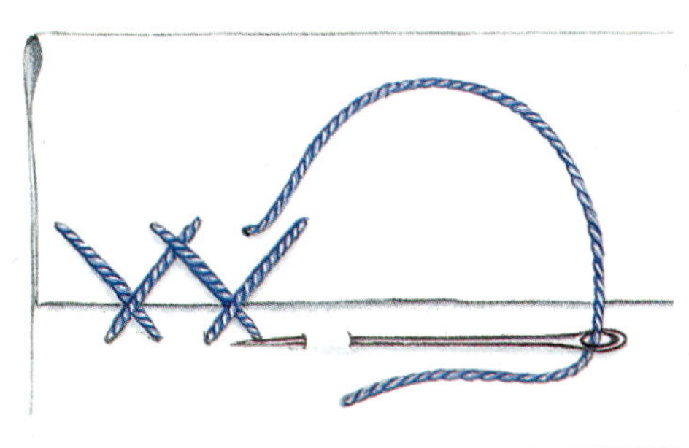

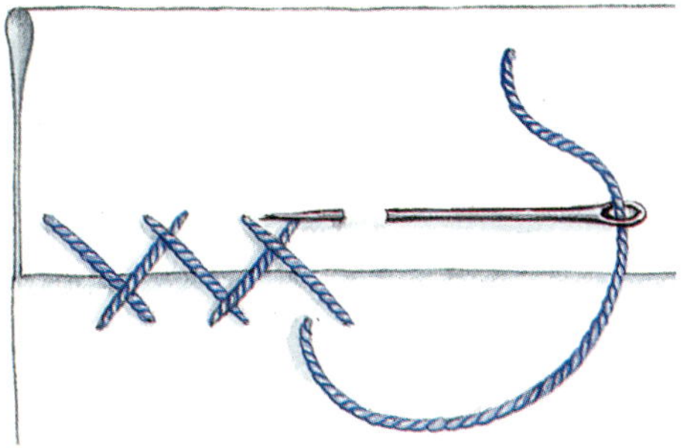

HERRINGBONE STITCH

A criss-cross stitch, worked from left to right but with the needle pointing from right to left, ideal for securing hems. (Also called catchstitch.)

LADDER STITCH

This is useful for matching patterns across fabric pieces when sewing a seam. If a normal seam technique was used, the pattern would be invisible – or showing only faintly through from the right side – and thus difficult to match precisely.

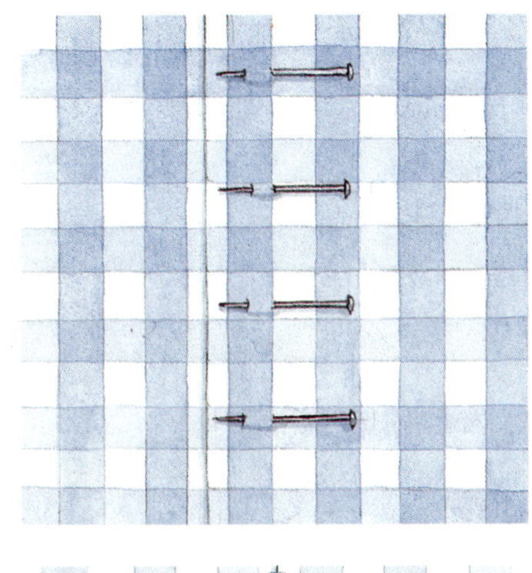

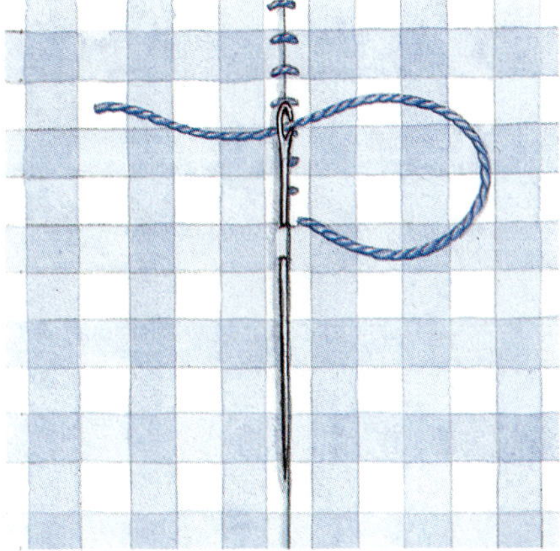

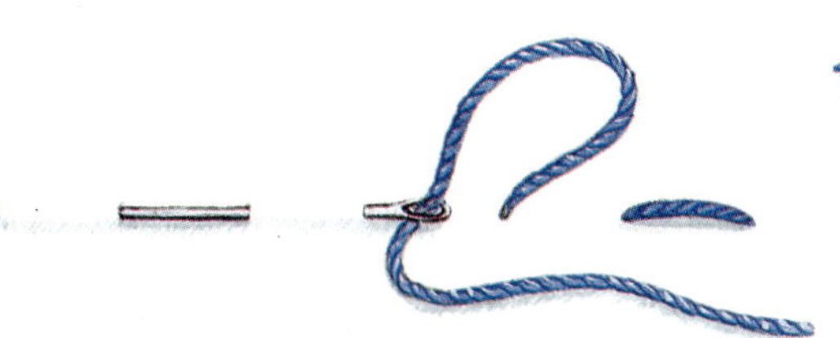

RUNNING STITCH

Worked by hand or machine, this is a useful quilting and gathering stitch.

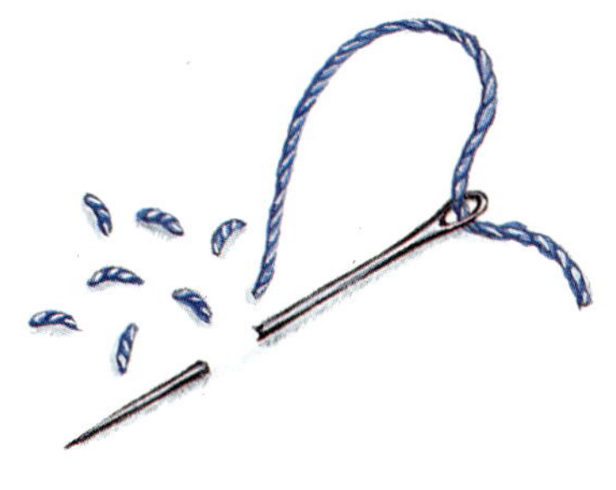

SEED STITCH

Small bar stitches, sewn randomly, can quickly and easily cover a wide area of fabric for a loosely embroidered effect.

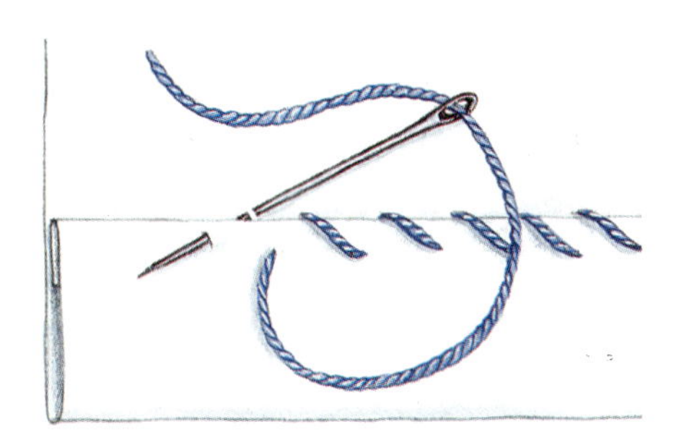

SLIP STITCH

By picking up just a few threads from the main fabric, this stitch makes nearly invisible hems. It can also be used to join two folded edges, as for mitred corners.

STEM STITCH

Make neat, even stitches, keeping the thread to the left of the needle, for a single line of stitching. For a looser effect, insert the needle into the fabric at a slight angle.

SUPPLIERS

UK

ARTHUR G. TAYLOR SAILMAKERS
Sail Lofts, Hythe Quay
Maldon, Essex
CM9 7HN
01621 853456

ARTHUR SANDERSON
100 Acres, Oxford Road
Uxbridge, Middx
UB8 1HY
01895 238244

CELIA BIRTWELL
71 Westbourne Park Rd
London W2 5QH
0171 221 0877

DESIGNERS GUILD
277 Kings Road
London SW3 5EN
0171 351 5775

HABITAT
0645 334433 for nearest branch

H A PERCHERON
97-99 Cleveland Street
London W1P 5PN
0171 580 1192

IAN MANKIN
109 Regents Park Road
London NW1
0171 722 0997

IKEA
0181 451 5566 for nearest branch

JANE CHURCHILL
151 Sloane Street
London SW1X 9BX
0171 730 9847

J W BOLLOM
15 Theobald Road
London WC1
0171 242 0313

LIBERTY OF LONDON PRINTS
3rd Floor Chelsea Harbour Design Centre
Chelsea Harbour
London SW10 0XE
0171 349 5500

MacCULLOCH & WALLIS
25/26 Dering Street
London W1R 0BH
0171 629 0311

MANUEL CANOVAS
2 North Terrace
Brompton Road
London SW3 2BA
0171 225 2298

MULBERRY HOME COLLECTION
The Rookery
Chilcompton
Bath BA3 4EH
01761 232876

PAVILION ANTIQUES
Freshford Hall
Freshford
Bath BA3 6EJ
01225 722522

THE BLUE DOOR
77 Church Road
London SW13 9HH
0181 748 9785

THE CONRAN SHOP
Michelin House
81 Fulham Road
London SW3 6RD
0171 589 7401

TURNELL & GIGON
20 Chelsea Harbour Design Centre
Chelsea Harbour
London SW10 0XE
0171 351 5142

WARRIS VIANNI
85 Golborne Road
London W10 5NL
0181 964 0069

AUSTRALIA

LINCRAFT (HO)
103 Stanley Street
West Melbourne
VIC 3003
03 9329 8555

SPOTLIGHT (HO)
100 Market Street
South Melbourne
VIC 3205
03 9690 8899

BARGAIN BOX FABRICS (HO)
22-24 Research Drive
Croydon
VIC 3136
03 9761 5500

CANADA

BB BARGOONS (HO)
201 Whitehall Drive
Unionville, Ontario
905 475 3172

FABRICLAND DISTRIBUTORS (HO)
76 Miranda Street
Toronto, Ontario
416 789 7841

BOUCLAIR HOUSE OF FABRIC STORES (HO)
400 Rte 132
Saint Constant, Quebec
514 635 8407

SOUTH AFRICA

THE FABRIC LIBRARY
61 Pretoria Road
Midrand 011 805 211

THE FABRIC LIBRARY CAPE TOWN
Oxford House Design Centre
11 Buitensingel Street
Cape Town
021 26 1501

THE ORIENTAL PLAZA
184 Main Road
Fordsburg
Johannesburg
011 838 6752

THE FABRIC WAREHOUSE
66 Mutual Village
Rivonia Boulevard
Rivonia
011 803 1133

With special thanks to all at Jane Clayton Associates, Margaret Bird, Melanie Williams and Penny Marshall for their superb sewing expertise.

The author would also like to thank the following for generously donating materials for use in the projects:
Arthur G. Taylor: Acrylic canvas (garden canopy, page 100) **Arthur Sanderson:** velvet (pleated curtains and cushions, pages 54 & 59) **Designers Guild:** 'Calico' chartreuse (reversible curtains, page 42); 'Sabuk' (wardrobe, page 116); 'Boula' graphite, putty (covered boxes, page 127); 'Oola check' lime (Roman blind, page 60); 'Rosa' lime (Garden canopy, page 105) **Habitat:** chair (page 30) **H A Percheron:** 'Minos' stripe (cushions, page 18); 'Tea Introduction' and stripe (screen, page 106) **Ian Mankin:** 'Dorset check' (reversible curtains, page 42); 'Atlantic stripe' (beach tent, page 112) **Jane Churchill:** 'Meadow check' (bed canopy, page 98) **J W Bollom:** flame-retardant felts (cushions, page 10) **Liberty of London Prints:** 'Mihrab' (dining chair cover, page 28); 'Minzah' (chair cover, page 33) **Manuel Canovas:** 'Vitry' check (laundry bag, page 46) **Mulberry:** 'Hedgerow' linen union (reversible curtains, page 42) **Turnell and Gigon:** 'Windsor' check (screen, page 110) **Warris Vianni:** Indian silks (bolsters and bags, pages 34 and 39)

INDEX